Arthur Miller's
DEATH
OF A
SALESMAN
and ALL MY SONS

JOAN THELLUSSON NOURSE
DEPARTMENT OF ENGLISH
ST. JOHN'S UNIVERSITY

MONARCH
PRESS

Published by
MONARCH PRESS
a Simon & Schuster division of
Gulf & Western Corporation
Simon & Schuster Building
1230 Avenue of the Americas
New York, N.Y. 10020

MONARCH PRESS and colophon are trademarks of
Simon & Schuster, registered in the U.S. Patent and
Trademark Office.

Standard Book Number: 0-671-00688-6

Library of Congress Catalog Card Number: 66-1851

Printed in the United States of America

CONTENTS

CONTENTS

INTRODUCTION

PULITZER PRIZE PLAYWRIGHT. For the 1948-1949 theatrical season Arthur Miller's *Death of a Salesman* was granted the coveted Pulitzer Prize. It also received the New York Drama Critics' Circle Award, the Antoinette Perry Award, the Theatre Club Award, and the Front Page Award, as well as general critical acclaim. The dramatist so honored was then only thirty-five years old, yet this was his third play produced on Broadway. The first, *The Man Who Had All the Luck* (1944), closed after four performances. The second, *All My Sons* (1947), was widely hailed, enjoyed a good run, and garnered some awards, such as that of the Critics' Circle. Such unusual recognition was accorded the young playwright because of his superior stage craftsmanship, his efforts to develop a new, modern type of tragedy, and his strong, serious concern with social issues affecting his fellow-countrymen.

TECHNICAL PROFICIENCY. Revealing early a talent for creative writing, Arthur Miller wrote several prize-winning plays at the University of Michigan and afterwards sold radio scripts, all the while perfecting himself in his craft. He especially admired Henrik Ibsen, the great Norwegian master of the "well-made," tightly constructed play. And both *All My Sons* and *Death of a Salesman* have carefully planned plots, wherein skilled use is made of such typical Ibsen devices as foreshadowing, irony, and symbols. Also observed are the traditional "unities," inasmuch as each has one main story line (unity of action) that develops in and about one small area, such as the hero's house (unity of place), within a brief two- or three-day period (unity of time).

If, however, both plays evidenced command of time-tested older stage methods, *Death of a Salesman* also strikingly employed certain techniques associated with later experimental writers. For instance, during the 1920s, those known as Expressionists had attempted to create special effects by freely shifting action from place to place and altering the customary time sequence. In *Death of a Salesman*, Miller actually does keep to standard chronological order and conventional home and office locales in depicting Willy Loman's last hours from his return to his house Monday night until his suicide late Tuesday. But the famous interposed flashback scenes, representing past experiences now preying upon Willy's distracted mind, cut across more rigid plot lines to achieve greater fluidity. Moreover, having the set itself designed for unhampered movement and the same actors playing characters in both current scenes and flashbacks further breaks down ordinary barriers, with clever lighting and background music making transitions easy and natural.

In addition, other modern dramatists, such as Eugene O'Neill, had engaged in noteworthy efforts to deal on stage with the curious inner workings of the human mind. In *The Great God Brown,* for example, O'Neill had used masks to convey the difference between the characters' surface behavior and their tormented inner selves, wracked by fear and anxiety. And in his *Strange Interlude,* he used spoken "asides," theoretically unheard by other characters in the same scene, again to deal with hidden worries and frustrations. Another well-known playwright, August Strindberg, of Sweden, had shown in his dramas how doubts and tensions could bring about madness or lead to suicide.

In *Death of a Salesman,* Miller lets us know not only what Willy says to his wife, Linda, and his son, Biff, but also what memories are causing him to become mentally disturbed. He uses flashbacks, however, rather than masks or asides to reveal how inner tensions can impel a man toward self-destruction. Hence, in handling his subject, he continues the comparatively recent trend of concentrating upon psychological aspects of character.

To sum up, those evaluating Miller's work, and particularly *Death of a Salesman,* were much impressed with his mastery of technical skills, noting that he combined to advantage the tight structure of the "well-made" Ibsen play with the free-flowing movement of the Expressionists and the psychological analysis favored by other experimental dramatists.

TRAGEDY FOR TODAY. When the ancient Greeks or Elizabethan playwrights, such as Shakespeare, wrote tragedies, they usually selected as hero an exceptional individual occupying a high, influential position. A basically good man, with some weakness in his character or "tragic flaw," the hero eventually falls from his great height of fame, wealth, power, and respect, to the depths of misery and often to his death. As Aristotle, the ancient Greek philosopher, indicates, audiences seeing this happen experience a "catharsis," or the purifying of the spirit, as they feel "pity" for the terrible woes of this admirable figure and "fear" because of an increased awareness of the forces in the world powerful enough to topple even the mightiest. Caught up in events of great magnitude, or so the theory goes, spectators are imaginatively liberated from all that is dull, petty, and mean in the life around them. Instead, they are stirred by the spectacle of human greatness, of Man daring to reach out beyond reasonable limits in quest of some glorious ideal. And even when he fails, as fail he must, there is still, for them, the satisfaction of having viewed nobility in action.

In sharp contrast, Miller's *Death of a Salesman* tells of no illustrious prince or general, but of an ordinary Brooklyn "drummer" (salesman), who has never been at any time rich or famous or in any way influential beyond the circle of his own family. In a sense he cannot "fall," in the way Greek or Shakespearean heroes could, because he has never occupied a high enough position. Moreover, his objectives are ostensibly not the most exalted. He wants to be well-liked, make some money, and have his two sons also be popular and prosperous. He is largely the "common man," with rather mundane aspirations, as opposed to the traditional extraordinary or unique hero, whose dreams were breathtakingly bold.

Arthur Miller has argued, however, that if tragedy has ever had any meaning for men in general, most of whom are not kings, it must have dealt essentially with thoughts and feelings that have some universality. And the common man of today, he maintains, can be just as much the good human being with a "tragic flaw" attempting against formidable odds to transform some vision into a reality. Even if he does not want to secure a throne like Macbeth or conquer the world like Marlowe's Tamburlaine, he can at any level give himself so completely to his own personal struggle that the very intensity of his passion tends to prove Man still indomitable. Willy Loman's craving to be a well-liked, successful salesman and family man may be as ordinary as that of Ed Keller in *All My Sons* to leave a thriving business to young Chris. But both men, although in somewhat blundering fashion, go after their goals with fearsome, uncompromising determination. And both in a general sense go to their deaths rather than live on as acknowledged failures. Doubtless, to some extent they are psychologically warped, but they are not merely maladjusted. To some extent they are victims of a social environment instilling faulty values, but this is not the complete explanation either. For good or ill, they are men who take a stand and hold to it regardless of dire consequences. And this total commitment, heroically maintained in the face of great personal tribulation, entitles such heroes as stolid Ed Keller or distracted Willy Loman, in Miller's view, to tragic status. And since their problems are today more genuinely meaningful anyway than those of the fast disappearing aristocracy, they may point a way, he maintains, perhaps the one possible way, in which tragic drama can elevate the spirit of the present generation.

In advancing such opinions, and carrying them out in his plays, Arthur Miller was advocating nothing completely new or revolutionary. Ibsen and O'Neill had dealt with tragic situations involving middle-class individuals; and from 1750 on through the whole Romantic period there had been much talk of the "common man." But Miller's plays were powerful, and Miller's statements strong and challenging. So his efforts on behalf of the "new" tragedy were regarded with respect and hailed as significant.

SOCIAL CRITICISM.   Arthur Miller was, of course, not the first American playwright to view critically certain values held by our people. Eugene O'Neill's works had some comments upon the American social scene, and such writers as John Steinbeck and Clifford Odets, Robert Sherwood and Maxwell Anderson had all contributed dramas with perceptive observations about life in this country. But many of the plays produced over the years on Broadway have been superficial and trivial. Indeed, the various groups giving awards for theatrical excellence have sometimes had to skip whole seasons for want of productions worth commending. Hence, the emergence of Arthur Miller as a serious social dramatist, as well as a superior craftsman and creator of tragedies, was regarded with enthusiasm.

Essentially, Miller criticizes first of all the sort of family-oriented morality that causes Americans to lose sight of their responsibilities to the larger social groups of which they are also members. Ed Keller, of *All My Sons,* behaves admirably to his immediate family as a good, hard-working husband and father. But to save the family business, he will ship out defective plane parts that may bring woe to other American families. Willy Loman would not presumably steal from his sons, Biff and Happy. But he is tolerantly amused when they appropriate footballs or building materials that belong to others. And Willy's boss, Howard, another apparently devoted family man, is callously indifferent to the fate of an aging long-term employee. Miller shows such social irresponsibility as leading to wartime profiteering on the home front and to ruthless competition in the business world generally.

Several other dubious aspects of life here also receive critical notice in his plays. He eyes skeptically, for instance, the over-emphasis upon a sort of facile surface charm, the big smile and glad hand, at the expense of more solid virtues. He notes the fantastic acclaim lavished on the muscular victors of the football field, and the contrasting rejection of equally muscular trades in favor of more "respectable" white-collar jobs, however spiritually unrewarding. He speaks out against the insistence upon getting ahead and surpassing others that works against good neighborly relations. Note how readily Ed Keller sacrifices the interests of his next-door friend and partner, and how insultingly Willy speaks to Charley. In later plays, Miller especially decries the smugness and narrow-mindedness that lead to deplorable acts of intolerance.

Again, Arthur Miller was not the only writer voicing such views. Ibsen and other dramatists abroad had long before this developed a type of theatre adaptable for criticizing the values and attitudes of modern society. But in combination with his other manifest achievements, Miller's serious endeavors as an American social critic won him, from the first, encouraging recognition on the part of all who felt that the contemporary stage should show concern for the problems of contemporary life.

EARLY YEARS. Born in New York City on October 17, 1915, Arthur Miller was the son of an Austrian-born clothing manufacturer. He grew up in Brooklyn, which he would use as setting for *Death of a Salesman* and *A View from the Bridge*. In both plays he notes changes occurring during the years of his youth. Willy Loman, for instance, saw the almost rural area of small houses with flower and vegetable gardens yield to tall apartment buildings. And Alfieri, the lawyer in the later play, saw its waterfront become more "civilized." Although Miller says little directly about his home life, there are some autobiographical hints in his plays. The genial side of Joe Keller may well have been suggested by his father's good-natured joking, and *After the Fall* indicates that his mother gave early encouragement to his literary promise.

DEPRESSION YEARS. Graduating from Brooklyn's Abraham Lincoln High School in 1932, Miller hoped to go to college, but the Depression had limited family finances. Several of his works reflect how hard men had to work to make a living during those years. Eddie, in *A View from the Bridge,* tells of his struggle to support his family, and it is clear that both Ed Keller and Willy Loman never found it very easy to forge ahead. In any event, to earn money toward a higher education, young Miller worked for two years in a warehouse supplying automobile parts. Certain of the more pleasant aspects of this experience he recalls in his short play *A Memory of Two Mondays.* Subsequently he was able to go on to the University of Michigan. There he won the Avery Hopwood Award for his first play, *The Grass Still Grows.* He then continued to write dramas, completing his college course by means of a part-time newspaper job and help from the National Youth Administration.

RECOGNITION IN NEW YORK. Returning East after his 1938 graduation, Miller continued to create plays, while holding various jobs to make a living. He is said to have worked in a box factory and the Navy Yard, to have driven a truck, waited on tables, and served as crewman on a tanker. He also was connected with the Federal Theatre Project, wrote scripts, and did research for a film. In 1944 he brought out a war commentary, *Situation Normal*, and in the following year he published a novel against anti-Semitism, called *Focus*. His first play to receive a Broadway hearing, as indicated previously, was *The Man Who Had All the Luck* (1944). But full-scale success was attained actually with *All My Sons* (1947) and *Death of a Salesman* (1949).

AMERICAN FAMILY TRAGEDIES. Both *All My Sons* and *Death of a Salesman* deal with the business and domestic problems of middle-class American families. Both concern a father in conflict with two sons whose love and respect he ardently desires. Ed Keller wants, above all, to leave his boys a thriving business. But one, Larry, dies in the war. The other, Chris, is appalled to learn that while he was fighting overseas, his father shipped out defective plane parts. Rejected and condemned by his surviving son, Keller commits suicide. Never so prosperous as Ed Keller, Willy Loman too has great hopes for his sons, especially the elder, Biff. Willy brags to both of his boys about his being well-liked and assures them of a great future awaiting them. Biff, disillusioned upon discovering his father's deceptions, drifts from job to job, while Happy resentfully makes up for his insignificant position by sensual self-indulgence. Unable to accept their failure and his own, Willy kills himself so that he can at least leave some impressive insurance money.

Of the two, *All My Sons* is the more conventional in form, with *Death of a Salesman* achieving fluidity by the skilled use of flashbacks. In both the heroes are not highly intelligent and not given to much genuinely perceptive self-criticism. They mean well, in general, but having uncritically accepted certain values find it hard to see where they went wrong. In both instances their sons come to reject their standards and angrily point out why. This means heartbreak for the older men, with Keller eventually seeing more of the light than Willy ever does. Dramatically there is good lively conflict in these father-and-son scenes, and through the opposed points of view Miller is able to make some telling comments upon twentieth-century American life.

THE SALEM CHALLENGE. In 1950, Miller paid tribute to Ibsen, whose work he admired, by adapting the latter's fiery play about a repudiated idealist, *An Enemy of the People*. This, however, closed after a short run, although several years later it enjoyed some success off-Broadway. In 1953 Miller offered a new original work, *The Crucible,* based upon the trials for witchcraft that occurred in Massachusetts in the 1690s. In the 1950s the term "witch hunt" was being widely used to describe contemptuously various investigations launched by Congressional and other groups to expose un-American activities. Since it was understood that Miller himself had little sympathy for such official inquiries, many sought to reduce his play to a simple allegory. Actually it is no mere propaganda piece, although there certainly is, by implication, criticism of the attitudes and methods of later interrogators. Subsequently Miller himself was to be called before a Congressional Committee headed by Senator Joseph McCarthy and even be convicted for failing to cite the names of those who formerly had engaged in radical activities. And his 1963 drama *After the Fall* would have more to say regarding such probes.

The Crucible, of which a more detailed analysis is provided in another of this series of review books, tells of the havoc wrought in early Salem when some restless young girls claim that witches are abroad in their village. Their leader, the beautiful and vindictive Abigail Williams, hopes for revenge against Elizabeth Proctor, from whose service she was dismissed after having had an affair with Elizabeth's husband, John. As more accusations are made, and many, including Elizabeth, are arrested, John Proctor joins with other sensible townsmen to try to stop the outrages. Charged himself and imprisoned, he must decide whether to live and make provision for his children even if this means swearing to a lie, or going to his death rather than deny the truth. He makes the second choice. Like Ed Keller and Willy Loman he thus makes a full commitment, but sees issues more clearly than they do. So his sacrifice is thus perhaps more meaningful. A noteworthy feature of this drama is the language used to suggest the blunt but forceful idiom of the early colonists. Miller adapts the speech of the times admirably to give his play a period flavor without making the quaint touches unnecessarily intrusive. As compared with *Death of a Salesman,* the form or structure is more conventional. But it is a powerful play, with exciting action and eloquent lines. It also suggests an admirable idealism, for such characters as the two Proctors and Rebecca Nurse make truly heroic decisions.

TWO SHORT PLAYS.   Two and a half years later, in September, 1955, Miller offered a double bill of two short works, neither of which was particularly well received. The first, *A Memory of Two Mondays,* was a brief mood piece remembering his youthful experiences in the auto-parts warehouse. The young office boy, Bert, who is working, as did Miller, to earn money for college, takes a friendly interest in the joys and sorrows of his fellow employees, while wondering how they go on seemingly content with routine work over the years. When he leaves, however, he is saddened to realize how readily they will forget him. Snatches of poetry and certain softening effects in set and lighting cast an almost romantic glow over the mundane happenings in the drab, dingy old factory.

As for *A View from the Bridge*, here Miller chose to deal with Brooklyn residents quite different culturally from those in *Death of a Salesman*. Again, however, the tone was tragic and conflict was developed between family members of two generations. Again the father figure would seek blindly to safeguard the future for the young, and again be rejected and go to his death violently. Eddie Carbone, a hard-working longshoreman, is overly fond of his wife's niece, Catherine. When the girl falls in love with Rodolpho, an illegal immigrant sheltered by the Carbone family, Eddie convinces himself that the marriage would not be a good one for Catherine. Unable to dissuade her, he eventually turns informer and dies in a knife duel with Rodolpho's irate brother. Like Willy Loman, Eddie is not overly intelligent and cannot perceive his bias even when enlightened by the wise lawyer, Alfieri. But once certain that his course is right, Eddie, too, gives full commitment. So he is another unyielding Miller hero, willing to give up everything for his tenaciously held belief. An interesting departure in this work is the use of the cultivated Alfieri as a sort of chorus, adding interpretations that could not be formulated by Eddie's uneducated group. And some critics have indicated other echoes in this play of older tragic themes. Yet again, this is a drama about a "common man," passionately determined and uncompromising. Dissatisfied with the work's original form, Miller later expanded the piece to a full-length play. Revived off-Broadway during the 1964-65 season, this longer form was hailed with enthusiasm as a strong, effective tragic drama.

AFTER THE FALL.   No new plays by Miller appeared during the next nine years until *After the Fall* opened at the new American National Theatre and Academy (ANTA) theatre in New York in 1964. During that time, however, significant events occurred in Miller's life. In 1956 and 1957, for instance, he was summoned before the McCarthy committee and found guilty of contempt of Congress. This conviction was later reversed. Also during this period he had marital difficulties. After a divorce from his first wife, Mary Slattery, by whom he had two children, he married in 1956 the well-known motion-picture star, Marilyn Monroe. With her in mind, he wrote a poignant story, *The Misfits*, and adapted it for the screen. She starred in the film with Clark

Gable. But this union, too, ended in divorce, followed by her suicide, and he subsequently wed a young European woman, Ingeborg Morath.

Like *Death of a Salesman*, *After the Fall* uses flashbacks to show what memories affect a man's thinking, but here all action takes place in the head of its hero, the lawyer, Quentin. There are no "outside" scenes, such as those between Linda and the boys, which are hardly in Willy Loman's thoughts. The setting is colorless and almost abstract. And characters appear and vanish readily as Quentin thinks about them. In general, Quentin, twice divorced and considering a third marriage to a German girl, reviews his life to date. He recalls unhappy scenes with his first wife, Louise. He painfully relives episodes occurring at the time old friends were summoned before Congressional committees. And above all, he keeps referring to his turbulent second marriage to an unstable blonde entertainer, Maggie, who later died a suicide. Agonizing over the problem of guilt, his own and that of others typified in Nazi atrocities, he finally takes heart from the counsels of Holga, the German girl, to accept his limitations and go on with courage and hope. The alleged autobiographical element in this work attracted considerable attention. In particular the rather sensational scenes with Maggie, the self-deceiving singer lost through drink and drugs, gave rise to comment. Some though the apparent revelations in poor taste; others merely found the episodes intensely dramatic. The over-all format too was the subject of controversy, some finding it too diffuse for any satisfactory development of plot or characters. Incidentally, Maggie's false image of herself recalls the instances of self-deception in *All My Sons*, *Death of a Salesman*, and *View from the Bridge*. And the scenes of family conflict from Quentin's boyhood echo the bitter domestic quarrels in earlier works.

INCIDENT AT VICHY. Also produced in 1964, this somewhat shorter work deals more fully with the question of Nazi crimes raised in *After the Fall*. In 1942, ten men suspected of being Jewish are brought in for questioning in Vichy, France. As the play proceeds, the ten prisoners speculate fearfully as to their fate, hopefully exploring every suggestion that all may yet be well. The final debate involves an intense Jewish psychiatrist who tries to convince an Austrian Catholic prince, arrested in error, that all who do not actively oppose the persecution of others are partially responsible for the resultant horrors. Appalled at this accusation, the prince gives his own pass to freedom to the doctor, thus accepting responsibility. Audiences in general seem to find this work a moving experience. The stakes are high, the suspense is continual, and the discussions are lively and revealing. Also interesting is the fact that with no intermission the action could realistically take place in the time allotted for the play. Adverse critics, however, have found little new said about the World War II atrocities and the ten "typical" characters little more than personifications of certain points of view.

SUMMATION. During the twenty years following his first Broadway production in 1944, Arthur Miller has remained in the forefront of important American playwrights. Most anthologies and histories of the drama in the country give space to his works, and productions of his plays have been given overseas. He has, of course, not escaped adverse criticism. His language has been called banal and lacking in emotional power. He has been attacked as too negative in his view of American society and especially unfair to American business. Again there have been those who have rejected his concept of tragedy as meanly bourgeois, regarding his "common man" heroes as "little" and "common" in the worst sense, and not genuinely human enough to qualify as tragic figures at all. Nor have his technical approaches been universally approved. *All My Sons* was found to be too rigidly constructed, *After the Fall* too diffusely. The Act One "Overture" to *The Crucible* has annoyed some commentators, and the terminal "Requiem" to *Death of a Salesman* others.

Yet the very prevalence of so much controversy over this dramatist testifies to his influential position in the American theatre. Regardless of objections posed to this or that individual aspect of his work, his reputation has remained unchallenged until recently (1964), when the critic Robert Brustein, among others, questioned Miller's worth as a dramatist. But even those who take issue with him have found admirable his continuing efforts to devise suitable new forms to express new and different themes. And among those who disagree with his literary, political, and social views are many who still find him a stimulating writer, one who at least does some thinking about vital contemporary issues. Finally, audiences for two decades have found his plays good theatre. They have wept over the death of poor, battered old Willy Loman and been awed by the plain-spoken, solid integrity of John Proctor. They have watched fascinated as deluded Eddie baits Rodolpho, they have listened with shock to the tirades of the embittered Maggie, and they have sympathized warmly with the diffidently heroic Austrian prince. Whatever else may be said, Miller commands the attention and stirs the hearts of most who come to see his dramas. And this gift is what most conclusively labels him a major playwright.

DEATH OF A SALESMAN

(1949)

CHARACTERS

WILLY LOMAN—The Salesman, over sixty, beaten and exhausted, who once dreamed that he and his sons would achieve success by being well-liked.

LINDA—His devoted and patient wife, who would have Willy's sons treat him with compassion and respect.

BIFF—Their older son, thirty-four, ruggedly built but disheartened, partial to outdoor farm work but afraid that it offers no future.

HAPPY—His brother, thirty-two, a slick, dapper clerk, who accepts bribes and brags about his sensual affairs, but talks of settling down with a good wife like Mom.

BERNARD—The slight, studious boy next door, who grows up to be a flourishing young lawyer.

CHARLEY—Bernard's father, an unassuming, quietly plodding businessman, who proves a loyal friend to Willy, "lending" him hundreds of dollars to salvage his self-respect.

UNCLE BEN— Willy's almost legendary older brother, whose talk of dazzling fortunes made quickly in Alaska and Africa filled the Salesman with tantalizing visions.

HOWARD WAGNER—The shallow, unresponsive son of Old Man Wagner, the original boss who had thought highly of Willy and predicted for him an eventual partnership in the firm.

JENNY—Charley's secretary, a little afraid of Willy when he seems overwrought and confused.

STANLEY—An accommodating waiter at Frank's Chop House, who is suitably impressed with Happy's bravado air of being a connoisseur of rare wines and beautiful women.

MISS FORSYTHE—An elegant, attractive young prostitute whom Happy suavely picks up in the restaurant.

LETTA—The girl Miss Forsythe obligingly provides for Biff, at Happy's request, an outgoing type who thinks Willy is "cute" and looks forward to jury duty.

THE WOMAN—A Boston buyer, whose casual affair with Willy did much to shatter young Biff's shining image of his father.

THE SETTING: Much of the "action" really occurs inside Willy's disturbed, faltering brain, as he relives crucial scenes from the past even while groping through present-day encounters. In general, however, the setting gives us the kitchen and two bedrooms of Willy's modest Brooklyn house, once practically suburban but now crowded in by high apartment buildings. Other locations, such as Howard's office, the restaurant, and the Boston hotel room, are set up on the stage apron with clever lighting and a few basic props. (The lighting involves the projection of a pattern of leaves on the stage during Willy's mental retreats from the present into the past, the density of the leaves indicating the extent of his withdrawal from reality, and the leaves themselves providing a symbolic reference to the more rural circumstances of the past.) Haunting flute music is used on occasion to set the mood, hopeful or plaintive.

PLOT ANALYSIS

ACT I. Wearily hauling in his big sample cases, Willy Loman, a salesman over sixty, returns unexpectedly to his Brooklyn home. En route to sell in New England, he tells his worried wife, Linda, he kept losing control of his car and had to come back. Linda urges him to ask Howard Wagner, his young boss, for easier work in town. She also tries cheering him with the news that their grown sons, Biff and Happy, are together again upstairs, amicably sharing their old room.

Willy is concerned about Biff, thirty-four, who has just quit one more farm job out West. How can such an impressive lad be so lost? Willy also regrets that their house, at last almost paid for, has been gradually hemmed in by soaring apartments. He misses the earlier country scents of spring flowers.

Upstairs, the boys, roused by Willy's arrival, laughingly recall their first flings with prostitutes. Then Biff, troubled, admits smarting under Willy's disapproval but says he found the routine of office and sales work too confining. He likes herding cattle better but fears that it offers no future. Happy, younger and cockier, can afford an apartment, a car, and the sensual affairs he craves. But he envies the highly paid merchandise manager, and gets even by taking bribes and seducing the fiancées of fellow employees. He would, however, like to settle down with a good girl like his mother. He is tempted by Biff's invitation to join him in some outdoor ranch project, but wants first to equal the manager as regards salary and prestige. Biff, in turn, talks of floating a loan from Bill Oliver, a sporting-goods man, whose employ he abruptly quit long ago after stealing a carton of basketballs.

Meanwhile, Willy, alone for a kitchen snack, relives a cherished memory. Young Biff and Happy, of high-school age, have proudly and energetically shined up the family car. Much pleased, Willy gives them a punching bag and is undismayed to learn that Biff has helped himself to a new football. The lads idolize him, and he boasts of his sales prowess. Young Bernard, the studious boy next door, warns that Biff is failing math and may not graduate. Willy scoffs at this, citing athletic-scholarship prospects. He predicts greater success for his sons since they are better liked than the conscientious Bernard.

A younger Linda enters with the wash. Having bragged to her of big sales, he quickly cuts his estimate when he learns how much they need for car payments and household repairs. He adds that he is not so sure of himself as he pretends. When Linda reassures him, his mind reverts guiltily to compliments paid him by a Boston buyer with whom he had an affair. He also is disturbed by new reports of Biff's wildness. Back in the present, Charley, Bernard's father, comes over to soothe Willy with a card game. Willy, however, remains nervous and irritable.

Something Charley says makes him recall his older brother, Ben. He remembers a brief visit when Ben told him of having made a fortune quickly in African diamonds. Ben also recounted how their father crossed the country with them in a wagon selling flutes. Actually, flute music is heard through much of the play. Ben urges Willy to try his fortune in Alaska and gives young Biff a lesson in fighting ruthlessly, jungle style. Charley warns that Biff is taking lumber from building projects, but Willy sees this as initiative. He sneers at Charley and Bernard as unable even to hammer nails.

Again in the present, Linda and the boys try getting the disturbed Willy to bed, but he insists upon taking a walk—in his slippers. Linda rebukes Biff for staying away and then quarreling with Willy. She loves her husband deeply, and feels that even if he is collapsing now he deserves respect as a person. His company, after thirty years, has taken him off salary and put him back on straight commission. The boys are shocked by this news and are saddened even more to hear that Willy has been trying

suicide. Once he drove his car off the road, and he keeps some
tubing handy, for inhaling gas. Biff promises reform, but upon
Willy's return they promptly argue bitterly. Willy, however, is delighted to hear of Biff's plan to approach Oliver. He tells him to
request a large sum and act as if he were already prosperous.
Biff and Happy talk further of organizing teams to sell a line
of sports equipment. Despite some further bickering, all are
buoyed up with hope: Happy says he will get married, Willy
will see Howard, and even the moon shines brightly on the little
house.

ACT II. The next morning, Willy, well-rested and confident,
prepares to face Howard. The boys have already left, with Biff
looking handsome and assured. Linda reminds Willy that they
need some two hundred dollars to cover the insurance premium,
repairs, and the last home mortgage payment. The house will
finally be all theirs, and Willy proudly recalls the good carpentering he did to make it strong and safe. Linda also gives him the
welcome word that his boys will take him to dinner that night.

At the office Willy can hardly get the attention of Howard, whose
one interest of the moment is a costly new tape recorder. Finally
made to listen, Howard disclaims a Christmas party pledge to
find Willy a New York job, and remains unyielding as the salesman desperately offers to work for less and less money. Angered,
Willy recalls an earlier business world in which selling roused respect and gratitude. Then old Dave Singleton, eighty-four, in green
velvet slippers, could sit in his hotel room anywhere and sell
buyers by phone. Howard will not hear of old promises made to
Willy by his father, and eventually discharges Willy, despite his
eagerness to try the Boston route again.

Again reverting to the past, Willy recalls Ben's urging to seek his
fortune in Alaska. Then, however, Linda had stressed the good
prospects in his selling job. He then relives the day of Biff's last
football triumph at Ebbets Field. Even Bernard pleads to carry
the shoulder guards, but Charley chides Willy, half-jokingly, for
letting a game mean so much at his age.

Back in the present, Willy makes a distractedly noisy entrance
into Charley's office, upsetting Jenny, his secretary. There with
luggage and tennis rackets is Bernard, now a pleasant, confident
young lawyer, off to try a case before the Supreme Court. After
pitiably bluffing about Biff's prosperity, Willy sadly asks Bernard
why Biff gave up. Puzzled himself, Bernard does know that Biff
really lost heart not after the math failure but after a trip to
Boston to meet Willy. This information disturbs Willy further.

He then asks for and receives a large sum from Charley but refuses the latter's well-meant offer of a job. His benefactor disputes the idea that success stems from being well liked, and also sharply denies that Willy would be worth more dead. As he leaves, Willy sobs that Charley is his one friend.

At Frank's Chop House, Happy impresses the waiter, Stanley, with his sophisticated airs and deftly picks up an attractive prostitute, Miss Forsythe. Then he sends her for a friend for his rich, notable brother.

Upon arrival, however, Biff glumly admits that Oliver had no time for his former shipping clerk. Upon impulse, Biff stole his fountain pen, but knows now that his life has been one great lie. Willy joins them, in no mood for Biff's facing of hard facts. Drifting again back into the past, he relives the distressing scene in which the idolizing Biff caught him in a hotel room with the lady buyer. Biff then angrily denounced his father as a lying fake and dropped plans for going on to any university.

In the present, coming back to the table after a trip to the men's room, Willy is dismayed to find boys and prostitutes gone. Hurt, he tips Stanley well and goes off, oddly, to buy seeds. Later, Happy and Biff return home with flowers for Linda. She is furious and orders both to leave home and stop tormenting their father. Out planting the old garden by flashlight, Willy discusses with the phantom of Ben the merits of killing himself and leaving the twenty thousand dollars of insurance for Biff. It would be a great gesture, and he would have a huge funeral. Ready to leave, Biff argues that Willy should never have filled him or himself with such blown-up ideas of their own importance. He, Biff, has just been in jail for stealing a suit. They quarrel further, but Biff breaks down. And Willy, convinced at last of his son's love, knows what he must do. Over Linda's fearful protests, he drives off in his car to kill himself.

REQUIEM. Charley, Bernard, and the three Lomans are the only mourners at Willy's grave. Linda grieves that he had to die just when the house was finally theirs. They talk of Willy's fine carpentering, and Charley envisions him as riding on "a smile and a shoeshine." Biff is leaving, but Happy still wants to make Willy's grandiose ideas work. Linda alone sobbingly asks Willy why he did it. They had their house and could now at last have been really free.

DETAILED SUMMARY AND ANALYSIS

ACT I, SCENE I

Willy Loman, an aging Brooklyn salesman, returns home exhausted and irritable late one Monday night. His loyal wife, Linda, is alarmed, for by now he should be in New England on a sales trip. He tells her, however, that he could not concentrate and kept driving his car off the road. She suggests that rest might help and urges him to seek office work near home. Their grown sons, Biff and Happy, amiably reunited, are asleep upstairs. Biff, thirty-four, has just come back from one more temporary farm job. Angered and concerned, Willy cannot see how so promising a youth can be so lost. He also regrets peevishly that their house, now almost paid for, has lost its country surroundings of grass and flowers and is now hemmed in by tall apartments. He muses about the happier past, back in 1928, when the smiling, popular young Biff used to polish so expertly their old red Chevrolet.

CHARACTER ANALYSES

In this opening scene significant aspects of Willy's personality are introduced, and several are effectively developed. A few of Linda's traits also are revealed, and there are brief descriptive references to the still unseen Biff, Happy, and the young boss, Howard.

WILLY. Willy appears first as a tired, worn man of sixty. His weariness is apparent in the hunched-over, stooped way in which he carries in his heavy sample cases. Besides, he himself says that he is weary, and Linda insists more than once that he needs rest and a less demanding job assignment.

He is also obviously shaken. His work as a salesman requires him to do a great deal of driving, and now he seems unable to keep his car under control. He rejects Linda's comforting assurance that it may be some easily solved problem, such as that of getting new glasses. And he is especially frightened when he realizes that although he was behind the wheel of his current Studebaker, he actually thought for a time that he was still steering the old red Chevrolet of 1928.

Thirdly, he is short-tempered. He answers Linda sharply, retorts angrily when accused of criticizing Biff, and is unreasonably irked to be offered whipped cheese instead of his customary Swiss. He testily complains about the unopened windows and condemns the builders of apartment houses for the ruining of the neighborhood.

In addition, he is worried, especially about Biff. Why has he not found himself some steady work and settled down? Is it mere laziness? Willy wants him to make a good living and is at a loss to understand why he cannot. This combination of anxiety and bewilderment has led Willy to greet his returning son with reproachful questions, and relations are strained between them. Willy also hopes that he is not causing Linda to fret, for she is his source of strength.

Finally, Willy reveals the wistfulness of a dreamer. This is emphasized subtly by the plaintive, light theme played on the flute as background music. Moreover, there is his delighted response to the pleasant scenery along the road, as well as his recollections of the lilac, wisteria, and peonies that used to give out a springtime fragrance before the apartment builders "massacred" the neighborhood. There is nostalgia, too, as he thinks of the smiling, popular younger Biff, who shined up the Chevrolet so beautifully that no one would believe it had gone eighty thousand miles.

LINDA: Willy's wife is shown here to be patient, tactful, and considerate. Even when the tired, peevish Willy is hard to please and replies rudely, she keeps her temper and tries to soothe him. Lovingly she takes off his shoes and makes every effort to restore his confidence in himself.

Yet she is clearly no mere passive helpmeet. She takes issue with Willy for talking so harshly to Biff and tells him to control himself. She would have him do nothing to dishearten further this troubled young man who is still trying to find himself. She also ventures to cut in on his tirade against the apartment builders with the remark that others have to live somewhere. Moreover, she is quite insistent that he see Howard about a less taxing position.

Although Linda, in general, murmurs reassuring words to Willy, she is shown from the first to possess a realistic awareness of the true situation. Her remark that Willy's "mind is overactive" is shrewdly perceptive, and she shows a sensitive appreciation of Biff's discouragement and confusion.

BIFF: Although only discussed here, Biff is represented as a cheerful, eager, well-liked boy who for some reason grew up to be a moody, restless young man. For over ten years now, he has gone from job to job and never made much money. That he still has some pride is hinted when Linda dodges the question of his apologizing to Willy. But that he is also sensitive is suggested by her statement that he was "crestfallen" after Willy criticized him. Her comment here also indicates that Biff admires his father and cares a great deal about the older man's opinion of him.

As for Biff's laziness, that question is left open. Willy seems undecided, and he recalls the boy Biff as energetically simonizing the car. Linda, on her part, denies that he is lazy. She describes him as "lost," but offers no helpful explanation as to how their son lost his earlier breezy confidence.

HAPPY: Virtually nothing is said of the younger son, Happy. He is clearly not on Willy's mind now and does not figure prominently in Willy's recollections, as shown up to now. He is merely said to get along well with his brother and to have taken him out with him on a date. Later it will be evident that Happy is a sensual young man, much given to casual love affairs. Here he is placed in the general family picture, but not accorded much importance.

HOWARD: Willy's young boss is the son of "old man Wagner," who held great hopes out to Willy and treated him well. With the encouragement of that masterly prince, Willy opened up the New England territory for the firm. The son, however, shows little appreciation, and this implied coldness will crucially affect Willy's life later in the play.

PLOT DEVELOPMENT: WILLY AND HIS JOB. Willy's difficulties with the car suggest that his job may be in jeopardy. Linda, for all her reassuring manner, suggests that being over sixty he cannot be expected to do so much traveling. At her urging, he agrees to go ask Howard for a New York assignment. But the references to Howard's unappreciative nature indicate that Willy may meet opposition.

WILLY AND BIFF. It is evident that relations are tense and uneasy between father and son. Remembering the smiling lively youngster Biff used to be, Willy is disgusted with the thirty-four-year-old moody drifter. Yet he does want to help Biff. So he promises Linda to hold his temper, and try to find the youth a selling job. If, however, Biff prefers to return West, he will let him go without rancor. These are good resolutions. But Willy is seen to be so irritable and impulsive that doubt is created as to whether or not further hostilities will be avoided.

TECHNIQUE. In later scenes Willy's mind will slip back to past scenes, and he will be seen talking to such memory characters as the young boy Biff or the now dead Uncle Ben. But such flashbacks might be confusing in the opening scene, when the characters are met for the first time. Even here, of course, Willy does drift back to earlier days. He thinks of his first years with the company, Biff's popularity as a boy, the former flower gardens around the house, and the 1928 car polishing. These recollections, however, are conveyed only through Willy's dialogue, with the music of the flute sometimes adding a touch of strangeness. In general, then, this first episode takes place clearly in the present and makes virtually no use of the interesting stage devices later employed to show memories being reenacted in Willy's disturbed consciousness.

IMPORTANT THEMES: "LOSTNESS." Willy says that for an instant while driving he could not remember the last few minutes. Again, he thought he was in the old Chevrolet instead of the current Studebaker. Literally, then, Willy has not known where he was—he has been lost. At sixty, moreover, he is clearly unsure of himself, worried about his job and about his son. If Biff, who cannot seem to find a satisfying way of life at thirty-four, is "lost," so, in another way, is his sixty-year-old father.

FATHER-SON CONFLICT. Willy cannot accept Linda's idea that life is a "casting off." Biff is no longer a small boy; he is a grown man thirty-four years old. Yet Willy, even meeting him at the train, angrily upbraids him for failing to succeed. He cannot stop thinking about Biff and Biff's problems and says that he will try to get him a job. Biff, according to Linda, is badly upset when his father criticizes him, but still keeps coming home, unwilling to make a break. These two men are thus extremely concerned about each other, but from the first there are also deep hostilities that will lead to more and more violent arguments.

CHANGED LIVING CONDITIONS. When the younger Willy and Linda first started making payments on their Brooklyn house, it was in a pleasant semi-rural area with grass and flower gardens. Vegetables, too, were grown in the back yard. Since then, however, tall apartment houses have been built that shut out the light so that plants will not grow and substitute unpleasant odors for the fragrance of lilac and wisteria. Willy's little house and the hammock he and Biff swung between the elms thus becomes the symbol of an earlier, more individualistic, more easy-going America. The big apartments in turn suggest to Willy a population "out of control" and the new "maddening" competition. Only a few buildings in a small area are involved here, but the playwright seems to suggest that the changes may be more or less typical in America.

CHANGED BUSINESS CONDITIONS. When Willy began selling for the Wagner company, he virtually "discovered" New England for them. As a young man he opened up whole new territories and was properly commended by his employer, a "prince," who was "masterful." Now, however, the business is under the direction of Howard, the old employer's son. Howard is not one to "appreciate" long, loyal service. This theme will be developed further as the play proceeds. The cold, impersonal tone of business today will be contrasted with the friendlier, more humane spirit of past transactions.

LAMENT FOR THE PAST. The tone of the play is often nostalgic. Here Willy looks back to better times when old Wagner was his boss and his house had a flourishing garden. He recalls how much admired the light-hearted Biff was as a boy and how beautiful the red Chevrolet looked when polished. The present, by contrast, is a time of darkness and suffocation, of weariness and bewilderment, of blighted hopes and bitter quarrels.

ACT I, SCENE 2

SUMMARY. Upstairs in their old bedroom, the two sons are roused by Willy's noisy mumbling. Both are worried about him but are soon cheerfully reminiscing about their early affairs with prostitutes. Biff is ill at ease, however, aware of his father's scorn. He also feels that he should have settled down, but he has hated the routine and competition of steady jobs, and the more pleasant ranch work he has found financially unprofitable. Happy, in turn, has his own apartment, his car, and his feminine conquests. But he, too, longs for outdoor muscular work. Biff envisions a ranch they could handle together, but Happy still wants first the prestige of a large income. Biff thinks he might obtain a loan from Bill Oliver, an early employer, whom he left after stealing some basketballs. They hear Willy again, and Biff denounces him angrily.

CHARACTER ANALYSES

This scene concerns the two Loman brothers almost exclusively. Only brief references are made to Willy and Linda.

WILLY. Heard by the boys to mumble about the mileage on the old Chevrolet and Biff's expert car polishing, Willy unnerves

Happy and infuriates Biff. The sons' comments point up the fact that Willy's odd behavior has been going on for some time and is getting worse. Recently, Happy sent his father to Florida for a rest cure, but to no avail. Happy confirms the impression created in Scene 1 that Willy is mainly upset about Biff's drifting from job to job.

LINDA. To Happy, Linda represents the type of admirable woman he would willingly marry, as contrasted with the girls of easy virtue with whom he regularly has affairs. His mother has high standards and is incorruptible. To Biff, however, Linda appears the victim of Willy's boorish, inconsiderate actions. He is incensed that she should have to listen to his father's wild outbursts. Linda, therefore, as viewed in this scene, is the ideal wife and mother to be shielded, if possible, from the graceless behavior of Willy.

BIFF. In Scene 2 Biff shows himself antagonistic toward his father, protectively concerned about Linda, comradely toward Happy, and confused and anxious as to his own future.

At first Biff is reticent about his attitude toward Willy, although referring to him with no enthusiasm. Then, looking glum, he asks Happy why his father always seems to view him mockingly. He angrily rejects, however, his brother's suggestion that he is the cause of Willy's erratic mumbling. Later when the latter's wild talk becomes more audible, Biff reacts with fury and contempt. His father seems then only a self-centered, doltish individual who causes Linda annoyance. Still, Biff appears momentarily grief-stricken when he hears Willy refer to the old car-polishing days. There is pain as well as anger in Biff's "sour" rejection of Willy.

His references to Linda are few, but she is clearly someone he loves and admires. Although it is Happy who says he would like to find a girl like his mother, Biff also wants one who is "steady" and has "substance." And it is quite possible that he, too, sees her as an ideal type. Certainly, he is furious that she should be subjected to Willy's noisy, rambling talk. Later it will become evident why Biff's grudge against Willy has made him especially sorry for his mother.

As regards Happy, Biff seems to be genuinely fond of his younger brother. He amusedly recalls the time years ago when he first took Happy out with him on dates with whores. And his dream is to take Happy back with him out West so that they run a ranch together. He could trust Happy and they could both enjoy the outdoor work.

In general, Biff seems to Happy to have lost his old good spirits and self-confidence. For one thing, Biff is dissatisfied with his life to date. For years now he has gone from one temporary job to the next, and this he feels is the irresponsible course of a boy, not a grown man. He believes that he should marry some good, steady girl and settle down in some line of work. In this view he is thus in substantial agreement with Willy.

Yet he is uncertain which way to turn. He has held various business jobs and found them suffocating. He hated the routine and the indoor confinement, and the strong competitive spirit also disgusted him. Yet he realizes that such work pays well and makes it possible for a young man to become established. On the other hand, he has found considerable satisfaction in the open-air ranch work he has done in the West. He likes, for instance, to see the young colts in the spring. But the pay is low, and there are small future prospects.

His one solution at the moment is to try to obtain a loan and buy a ranch. In this way he could do the type of work he likes and still have some stability. He plans to approach a former employer, Bill Oliver, for the loan. Here his thinking seems somewhat fuzzy. For he quit Oliver's company shortly after stealing a carton of basketballs, and he thinks that Oliver suspected the truth. It is thus not at all clear why Oliver should lend such a dubious risk several thousand dollars. In terms, however, of Biff's mentality, the move is curiously plausible. Oliver, who once used to trust Biff, did tell him to ask him if he ever needed anything. This may well have been merely a conventional form of polite farewell, but the Lomans, both Willy and Biff, place much emphasis upon the personal bond in business. Despite all evidence to the contrary, their concept of economic relationships seems constantly to stress a man-to-man, informal, friendly meeting of individuals. Willy will talk to Howard, and all will be well. Biff will go back to the businessman who a decade or so ago put a reassuring hand on his shoulder, and will walk out with a ten-thousand-dollar loan.

Two other factors enter into Biff's vision of Oliver. Both identify Biff again as truly Willy's son. One is a streak of buoyant optimism that is hard to erase. Charley, a neighbor, will later eulogize Willy as a salesman "riding on a smile and a shoeshine." At this time in their lives both Willy and Biff are unhappy and discouraged. Yet every so often each suddenly feels an upsurge of confidence. Here, even to think of floating such a large loan from his ex-employer, Biff must have some of this hopeful enthusiasm.

There is also, however, ironically an underlying sense of desperation. Like his father, Biff at this point is beaten. He does not know what to do or where to turn. So almost any possibility that occurs to him will be seized upon with almost feverish concern. Only a man brought up to "think big" and concoct grandiose schemes could dream up the Oliver loan project. But Biff, who actually does voice misgivings, has no other prospects at all. So he will have to convince himself that Oliver did at least formerly think the world of him and may still be willing to hand him a sizable sum.

HAPPY. Like his father and Biff, Happy is described as a strong, muscular, athletic type. He holds a reasonably well-paid job in a store, but by no means finds the work itself satisfying. He, like his brother, would rather use his muscles and take on more strenuous activities in the open air. Yet he is not likely to accept Biff's invitation to join him out West.

Never Willy's favorite, Happy, the younger son, wants the respect and prestige that a lucrative job will guarantee. When the high-salaried merchandise manager enters the store, "waves part in front of him." Those who give Happy orders at work are not only "common" and "petty," but "pompous" and "self-important." Happy is determined to show them that he, too, can achieve success on their terms.

Happy, in brief, wants what his bosses possess, all the while regarding them personally with contempt. His own assumption that he is superior seems to have three bases. First of all, although this will be more apparent later, Willy always suggested that his sons were destined for greatness. As Biff says in this scene, they were not brought up to "grub for money." Secondly, Happy is very conscious of his physical strength and prowess. He thus resents being ordered around by those who cannot box so well, run so fast, or lift such heavy weights. Thirdly, he is proud of the fact that women find him attractive. He has even been able to seduce the fiancées of three store executives. He must therefore, in his view, be more virile and impressive than they are.

At the same time, he recognizes certain other deplorable aspects of his present way of life. For one thing, he is aware that material wealth does not in itself assure contentment. The merchandise manager, whom he envies, built an impressive house on Long Island, only to move out and start another within a few months. And even Happy, who can at least boast of his own apartment, his own car, and a steady supply of admiring women, admits he is often lonely and dissatisfied.

In addition, he does not like the intensely competitive spirit. If he were with someone like Biff, whom he could trust, he might be able to live up to his ideals. He would presumably be honest and would not tempt the fiancées of other men. Instead he would settle down with a good, dependable girl like his mother. As it is, all around him are corrupt, or so he claims. Hence, he takes bribes from buyers, ruins the future wives of his bosses, and eyes his fellow-workers with smoldering hostility.

A fairly sensual man, he apparently has many casual love affairs. He gets some pleasure from these dubious romances, and in addition, they help provide temporary escape from loneliness and frustration. They make him feel popular and important, and—especially when the girls are the other men's fiancées—more attractive than business rivals. Yet he must admit that often there is little thrill obtained from such brief relationships. And he feels vaguely guilty about his continual self-indulgence. So he tells Biff that what he really wants is marriage with a nice, respectable girl. Yet in order to change, he would, of course, have to give up the affairs. And while these have not given him the deeper rewards of a permanent relationship, they have helped to serve as some compensation for his decidedly subordinate position at work. They act as props to Happy's ego; and despite his repeated assurances of imminent reform, he will not readily do without these minor triumphs.

Happy is not altogether ungenerous. He seems to have financed Willy's brief and unavailing Florida rest cure. And here he is not without some concern for his father's worsening condition. Yet he was never the favored son, and he is not so emotionally shattered by the situation as is Biff. He asks Biff's help because Willy's behavior is "getting embarrassing." Biff is more likely to think of his mother's sufferings, but Happy, in general, is used to looking out mainly for himself.

PLOT DEVELOPMENT.   Most of this scene is taken up with exposition regarding the personalities and histories of the two sons. The only important plot element introduced here is Biff's plan to ask Oliver for a loan. This scheme will eventually have a crucial bearing upon relations between Biff and his father and will help bring about Willy's last momentous decision.

TECHNIQUE.   This scene, too, is essentially one of straight dialogue. During the boys' conversation, Willy can be heard apparently addressing the boy Biff who long ago so expertly simonized the car. But there is no dramatized flashback episode here. This scene's function is essentially to introduce two more main characters, and there is little evidence of any unusual or startling stage devices. Actually, of course, having a set that shows more than one room makes it possible to show Willy muttering in the kitchen while the boys talk upstairs. But the time sequence is normal, and events are occurring objectively, not solely in Willy's mind.

IMPORTANT THEMES: LOSTNESS.   Neither Biff nor Happy is really, contented. At thirty-four, Biff has no job and only the most doubtful of prospects (the Oliver plan). The outdoor work he likes offers no security and no future. The steady job that pays well has never held his interest long. He does not know what to do next. Happy is better established. He has a fair position, a car, and an apartment. But he feels that all is false around him and that he is constantly going back on his principles. Beneath his air of jaunty assurance, he, too, is anxious and confused.

FATHER-SON CONFLICT.   As regards Willy, Biff appears here both "sour" and concerned as well. Toward the end, however, hearing Willy's noisy mumbling, he becomes furious at his father for disturbing his mother. Happy, too, is worried about Willy but is also annoyed because the older man's erratic behavior is "embarrassing."

CORRUPTION IN MODERN BUSINESS.   Husky men both, Biff and Happy prefer working with their muscles in the outdoors. Both object to the confinement and routine of store or office work. Such attitudes may be merely matters of individual temperament, rather than indications of some flaw in the over-all system. Yet throughout there is some suggestion that the wilder, freer life of those who earlier pushed Westward offered greater satisfactions to the strong individual who was good with his hands. In the indoor world, according to the resentful Happy, meaner, commoner types give orders to those whose physical prowess they could not hope to match.

Both Biff and Happy also criticize the intensely competitive spirit of business. Biff can never see why he must always try to get ahead of the next man. Happy feels that this sense of competition drives him to seduce the fiancées of store executives. Yet while he deplores this emphasis, noting that getting ahead does not guarantee bliss, he still wants to prove his worth by making more money than the merchandise manager. The brothers wish they could be business partners. Each then would have someone to trust, and they would presumably be working *with*, not *against* each other.

Taken as a whole, the views expressed by Biff and Happy are not, of course, necessarily those of the playwright. These two young men have rather obvious personality flaws. Neither is exactly a mature, sensible, truly adult individual. When, for instance, Happy sneers at his fellow employees, he is probably revealing more about his own faults than about theirs. Yet there is sufficient stress upon the coldly competitive spirit in the business world, here and elsewhere in the play, to suggest that this may be Miller's observation.

COUNTRY VERSUS CITY. Nineteenth-century Romantic poets, such as William Wordsworth, wrote that those who lived in the country, close to Nature and its wonders, were likely to be happier, nobler. people than those forced to endure the ugliness of crowded cities. Here Biff's lyrical talks of the Western farm in the spring, with fifteen fine new colts, contrasts with Happy's disgruntled account of the competition, bribery, and questionable love affairs that characterize his urban world. It will be remembered that Willy remembers pleasantly the more rural Brooklyn of sweet-smelling flower gardens and feels stifled in the new city atmosphere of tall apartments with more and more people.

ACT I, SCENE 3

SUMMARY. Willy, downstairs, urges an unseen young Biff to finish his education before taking any girl seriously. But Biff's popularity pleases him. Praising both lads for their work on the car, he is joined on stage by his sons in high-school garb. Just back from a trip, Willy surprises them with a new punching bag. Biff, in turn, displays a new football, stolen from the locker room. Willy, laughing, commends his daring. Willy himself will some day own his own business, bigger than that of their neighbor, Charley, who is less "well-liked." He tells of greeting the Mayor of Providence and promises the boys a summer ride through New England with him. The big football game is set for Saturday, and Biff pledges a special touchdown for Willy.

CHARACTER ANALYSES

This scene reveals more of the personalities of Willy and Biff, with some brief glimpses of the younger Happy.

WILLY. The episode which Willy now relives occurred some fifteen years before. The fact that it is now uppermost in the salesman's troubled mind indicates the kind of life experiences that have most affected him.

First of all, it shows vividly how much he enjoyed the chance to be with his sons and to do things with them. From his admiring words to both, he thought highly of them. He taught them how to polish the car. He planned to have Biff help him chop down an overhanging branch threatening the house. He hoped to have them swing a hammock with him between some trees. He brought them a new punching bag and regaled them with his travel experiences. He was glad when they missed him and wanted their company on a summer trip along his route.

Willy is thus pictured as the devoted "family man," perhaps excessively devoted. As a traveling salesman, he was, of course, away from home a great deal. So he would undoubtedly welcome the opportunity to get together with his sons, of whom he was so proud. Yet there is here, on the part of both father and sons, an extraordinary degree of mutual affection and concern. For strapping high school boys to claim that they missed their father every minute he was away involves either exaggeration or a somewhat unusual relationship. And Willy, in turn, clearly made them, and especially Biff, his primary interest. This revelation is important because the lives of both Willy and Biff will be tragically disturbed when a break occurs between them.

Secondly, Willy is represented as a man who is capable with his hands. He gives them good, practical instructions about the care of the car. He suggests how they will remove the branch and how they will put up the hammock. He is also enthusiastic about this type of work and conveys pride in doing it well.

Thirdly, Willy places great stock in physical fitness. He does not bring his sons home a book or a science kit. He buys them a punching bag, excellent "for timing." He also talks of the advantages of jumping rope, and is keenly interested in the coming football game.

Furthermore, Willy is convinced that popularity is a strong index to success. He is delighted that the girls will even pay for the chance to be with Biff. And he is overjoyed that the coach likes Biff and that the team has chosen him captain. He suggests that the business he will someday own will be more impressive than that of their neighbor, Charley, because he, Willy, is better liked. And he emphasizes this quality in telling the boys about his New England route. He has been greeted by the Mayor of Providence. He has friends in every town. All like him and will welcome his sons when he brings them along. Even the police do not ticket his car because they recognize and respect him. Actually, Willy is bragging. He will tell Linda on another occasion that he often fears that others are laughing at him. But even if here he is engaged in wishful thinking, it is clear that he wants very much to be highly regarded. And his query as to whether or not the sons were lonesome for him indicates his desire to be well liked at home as well.

If, however, he instills in his sons the importance of personal popularity, he is not at all emphatic about the need for personal integrity. When he learns that Biff has taken the football, he tells
him to return it. But he is laughing at the time and is clearly not
much upset about the theft. Biff needs the ball for his practicing,
and the coach will hardly disapprove. Others might be censured,
but the well-liked Biff can get away with anything. Subsequently,
Biff declares he will make a special touchdown for Willy. According to Happy, Biff is not supposed to do this. He has been instruct-
ed to pass. But again Willy is delighted with the intended gesture.
If the boys are being given values by Willy, they are not being
taught to respect the property rights or authority of others. Later
we will find that Biff goes on stealing and that Happy accepts
sizable bribes.

Finally, Willy reveals once more his optimistic nature. The car
looks fine after the polishing, and the hammock will be hung
just right. The coach will understand Biff's "borrowing" of the
football and will even commend his "initiative." Someday Willy
will have his own business. Meanwhile, he can take the boys on
a wonderful trip. All the cities that he visits are beautiful, historic
spots, with friendly, admirable people. Given even faint hopes,
Willy tends to respond with enthusiasm.

BIFF.   This scene emphasizes Biff's strong affection for his father,
his popularity in school, and his rather questionable moral values.

Biff works hard on the car, obviously eager for Willy's praise. He
is delighted with the present of the punching bag and speaks of
missing his father "every minute" while the latter was in New
England. He listens appreciatively to Willy's stories and is eager
to go with him on the projected summer trip. He will not be
worried about the big game if his father is present. And he will
even go against orders to make a special touchdown just for Willy.

His popularity is suggested by the rumor heard by Willy that the
girls are paying to go out with him. He is also captain of the
football team, and the coach, at least according to Biff, is always
encouraging him. He is sure of himself and not worried at all
about the stolen ball. The fact that he is so casual about admitting
the theft suggests that he is not given to guilt feelings about such
moral lapses. He intends to return it anyway, he says angrily,
when accused. Biff's habit of taking things, shown here, will later
lead him into serious trouble. For instance, he will have to leave
Oliver's employ after taking a carton of balls.

HAPPY.   As compared with Biff, the young Happy receives little
attention from Willy. He does tell Happy to follow Biff's lead in

polishing the car, and he does throw him a word or two of praise. In general, however, Happy seems here as elsewhere to be trying to attract some attention. He lies down and pedals with his feet to show how he is losing pounds. And his "you notice, Pop?" seems to be a cry for more of Willy's regard. Willy does respond but without any continued interest. Hence, there will never be the closeness between them that develops between Willy and Biff.

CHARLEY.   This next-door neighbor is mentioned here as already possessing his own business. Willy, however, does not seem impressed. Charley is not sufficiently well liked to achieve the kind of success of which Willy dreams. The contrast between the two men will be developed further in later scenes.

PLOT DEVELOPMENT.   Since this is a flashback scene, it will not be as obviously one that advances the story as, for instance, those having to do with the efforts of Biff to see Oliver. Yet certainly Willy's vivid, overwhelming recollection now of earlier, less troubled times represents a further move toward his impending death. The painful contrast with the troubled present will increase the emotional strain. And gradually such memories will force him to live again with anguish a subsequent related episode that wrecked his close relationship with Biff. There is also, of course, exposition here. Biff's later stealing becomes more comprehensible in the light of his earlier, laughingly condoned purloining of the football.

TECHNIQUE.   This scene is the first of the play's now famous flashback episodes. Special lighting and a thin, transparent curtain, or scrim, are often used to distinguish these past events from those going on outside of Willy's mind at the present time. There has been a lapse of some fifteen years since the car polishing and the big game actually took place. Thus all the characters in such scenes were, naturally, that much younger. Yet the same actors play the roles at both ages. The younger Linda, when she appears, will wear a ribbon in her hair. The sons, when of high-school age, will wear appropriate sweaters. Much, however, will be suggested by the skilled use of voice and gesture. Willy, for example, hunched over with weariness when he first enters with his suitcases, will walk with a springier step and use more confident tones as the earlier, less harassed salesman.

One vital distinction must be made. To some extent the scenes from the past provide exposition—necessary information to make the present action intelligible. Yet, in a very real sense, they, too, are part of the present action. They represent the memories that currently are plaguing the distressed Willy and hastening his final crack-up. Willy is collapsing mentally and emotionally, and these particular recollections, in which he loses himself completely to the horror of his family, are very real factors in his progress toward self-destruction.

One other question may be raised. These being the memories of a confused, unhappy man, how accurately do they record what actually occurred long ago? There is evidence that Biff was once very fond of his father, that Biff was a school athlete, and that Biff did steal. Yet it is virtually impossible to determine whether or not Willy has distorted the over-all picture, and, if so, to what extent. All that can be stated positively is that this is what Willy's mind remembers and that this is the way the past seems to him. All in all, such scenes probably reveal more about Willy's psychological processes than they do about the factual history of the Loman family.

IMPORTANT THEMES: IMPORTANCE OF BEING WELL LIKED. Willy is most enthusiastic about Biff's popularity and makes a slurring reference to Charley as not being liked well enough. Biff, being highly regarded, will get away with the football theft. Willy, being well thought of, will have a greater business than that of Charley. Willy's account of his recent New England trip lays stress upon the friendly reception he is always given in the cities along his route. He intimates that popularity is the key to success.

IMPORTANCE OF PHYSICAL PROWESS. Willy buys the punching bag and tells Happy that jumping rope will help his timing. He is clearly interested in the upcoming football game. In addition, the car-polishing, branch-cutting, and hammock-slinging activities mentioned are all essentially physical.

IMPORTANCE OF FAMILY TIES: Both father and sons reveal intense affection. The boys miss Willy greatly when he is away, and are eager for his praise. He wants only to take them along on his route and show them off to his New England friends. He will brag about Biff's football prowess in Boston.

QUESTIONABLE MORALITY. Willy tells Biff to return the stolen ball but tends to condone his action. For one thing, Biff needed the ball in order to practice. Secondly, the theft showed independence or daring. Finally, Biff can get away with it because the coach has a high opinion of him. In later scenes, there will be other examples in which Willy shows this same lax attitude toward obviously censurable conduct.

SYMBOLS. In various of Miller's works certain objects shown or mentioned are used to point up significant themes. In this scene the following should be noted:

THE CAR. The old Chevrolet which Biff has polished is, of course, Willy's means of carrying on his job. But here it points up the close cooperation and friendly relationship between father and sons.

THE HAMMOCK. Together with the tree trunk that must be lopped off, the hammock first recalls the countrylike atmosphere later to disappear. It is also to be one more present brought home by Willy to his beloved sons. Finally, they will put it up together—hence, it is another family project.

THE PUNCHING BAG. This is a gift indicating Willy's continual interest in his sons. He always brings them home something. It also suggests Willy's concentration upon their physical development.

THE FOOTBALL. The stolen ball, of course, ties in with Biff's preoccupation with sports. It also is used to show how dubious are some of his moral values.

ACT I, SCENE 4

SUMMARY. As Willy's memories continue, young Bernard, Charley's son from next door, enters to warn Biff that if he does not pass mathematics he will not graduate. Willy sneers at the studious, bespectacled Bernard as anemic. Willy tells Biff to study, but is not seriously concerned. Bernard, he says, may get better marks, but Biff will be offered scholarships and succeed even as well as Willy in New England because the Lomans make a good appearance and are well liked. Happy again claims that he is losing weight by pedaling.

CHARACTER ANALYSES

WILLY. Here Willy again insists that being popular and making a good impression guarantees success. He does not tell Biff not to study. He does send him over to work with Bernard. But he is clearly convinced that the handsome, athletic Biff will get what he wants without much intellectual effort. Bernard works much more earnestly and gets much better marks. But, in Willy's view, this pale, slight lad who wears glasses and is not extremely "well liked" will never have Biff's chance to forge ahead in business. As the play proceeds, it will be made clear that Biff actually fails and Bernard succeeds. This fact will distress and bewilder Willy, but as a younger man, he is quite certain as he counsels his sons.

To make his point here Willy boasts of his own sales record in New England. Once his name is mentioned, all the buyers gladly see him. And he has made great sales in Providence and Boston. Later he will admit to Linda that the trip was arduous and the returns relatively small. Why, then, does he paint here such a false picture? It is possible, of course, that in a momentary burst of enthusiasm he actually believes what he says. He is carried away with his own theory of the importance of popularity and thinks of himself as a shining example. In addition, he always seems to be courting the love and admiration of his sons. So he probably always wants to play the hero before them. With Linda, by contrast, he sometimes lowers his guard. Finally, it is at least possible that for all his bluster, Bernard's dire predictions have shaken him slightly. His scornful references to the anemic young neighbor and his glorifying of the Loman breed of muscular, personable men may be thus essentially defensive.

BIFF. Bernard says that Biff will fail mathematics and lose his chance to graduate if he does not study. Biff neither denies nor accepts this well-meant warning. Instead he seems determined to evade the issue. He shows his father how he has printed University of Virginia on one of his sneakers. He brings up the matter of Bernard's limited popularity. And he changes the subject, asking about his father's trip. He seems to have accepted Willy's values as regards the importance of being popular. He also exhibits some of Willy's dubiously grounded optimism. The name of the university is printed on his sneaker. So, of course, he is on his way. The other unpleasantness will somehow be avoided.

HAPPY. There are here two brief revealing glimpses of Happy. The first occurs when he roughly, teasingly spins the less brawny Bernard around. This is the same Happy who will later be outraged that he must take orders from weaker men whom he can outbox and outlift. And again Happy is seen pedaling and trying to get Willy to note his loss of weight. Once more Biff has been the center of attention, and Happy seems to be begging for his share.

BERNARD. In his first appearance, Bernard is seen as a thin, far from husky young man, who wears glasses. He has no cause to fear about his own marks. He may well have, as Willy says, the best grades in the school. But he is fond of Biff and worries about his friend's future. Sneered at by Willy and taunted by Happy, he still comes to offer Biff his services as math coach. Considering the cool reception he gets, he shows remarkable patience and loyalty.

PLOT DEVELOPMENT. This memory of how he reassured Biff and spoke disdainfully of Bernard will undoubtedly help unsettle Willy still further when later he encounters Bernard as an assured, prosperous young lawyer at a time when Biff has no career at all. The matter of Biff's weakness in mathematics will also lead to the crucial subsequent Boston episode, which in turn will torment Willy and help drive him to his death.

TECHNIQUE.   This is another of the flashbacks and is handled in the same way as the previous scene.

IMPORTANT THEMES: IMPORTANCE OF BEING WELL LIKED.   Biff is better looking and better liked than Bernard, says Willy. So Biff will forge far ahead of the more studious Bernard once both are out in the business world. Willy himself succeeds in New England, he claims, because people are always glad to see him. "Be liked and you will never want."

IMPORTANCE OF PHYSICAL PROWESS.   The scornful references to Bernard as "anemic" and to the Loman boys as "Adonises" point up Willy's concept of the advantages possessed by the man of strong physique. Happy, too, tries to claim some notice by the physical activity of pedaling and the claim of losing weight for greater fitness. Both sons, when grown, it will be remembered, make much of their muscular virility.

IMPORTANCE OF SUSTAINED EFFORT.   Willy seems to have a certain contempt for Bernard's excellent marks. He dismisses him as a "pest." But the play will trace Bernard's success as contrasted with the confused floundering af all three Loman men. There is thus the implication that in the modern world, Bernard's course was the more likely to provide security, advancement, and certain other rewards.

QUESTIONABLE MORALITY.   Willy seems undisturbed by the news that Biff has not been studying. The school would not dare fail anyone whose athletic achievements had led to offers of scholarships to several universities. Biff could get away with the football. So he will get away with poor grades.

FAMILY SOLIDARITY.   Bernard, of course, represents a course of action opposing that of Willy. But it does seem that the three Lomans rather clannishly close ranks against him. The husky, well-liked Adonises, admiring each other, band together against the outsider.

SYMBOL: BIFF'S SNEAKERS.   Biff's sports shoes, with the University of Virginia carefully printed on the sole, represent his confident dream of a bright future through athletic scholarship. When this is shattered, the sneakers will be destroyed in a fit of angry bitterness.

ACT I, SCENE 5

SUMMARY.   As Willy goes on remembering, he is joined by the younger Linda, with ribbon in hair, carrying some wash. Willy sends the boys to hang it on the line, and Biff is helped by the school crowd whom he leads. Willy boasts to Linda of enormous sales but finally admits his commissions will not run above seventy dollars. Yet they must have over a hundred for household repairs. Willy is discouraged and unsure of himself. Linda flatters him reassuringly, and he is reminded of a Boston woman with whom he had an affair. He gave her stockings and the woman promised to get him in to see the buyers.

CHARACTER ANALYSES

WILLY.   Willy here is extremely proud of Biff, when he hears him ordering around the other lads. He takes credit for training him to be a leader and promptly goes on to preen himself on his own extraordinary sales work. As Linda probes, however, he lowers his estimates drastically and reaches for the excuse that the stores were taking inventory. Next time, however, he will do better.

Faced with the mounting bills for car and refrigerator, washing machine and roof repair, Willy suddenly seems to lose all the air of bravado he puts on before the boys. He is not at all sure that everyone likes him. Some do not pay heed to him at all, and others find him ridiculous. He is afraid that he talks too much, unlike Charley for whom they do have regard. Instead of being strong and godlike, he feels pudgy and fears that he looks foolish. He must work long hours for a discouragingly small return, and he gets very lonely on the road. Recalling this loneliness, he has the guilty recollection of being unfaithful to the loyal Linda with a Boston woman.

When Willy talks like this, audiences may well wonder which is the *real* personality. Is he deliberately lying to the boys? Is all the boasting a desperate attempt to mask his sense of frustration and failure? Or are these the quickly changing moods of a mercurial individual?

Certainly Willy is given to rapid shifts in judgment. In the opening scene one minute he suggests that Biff is lazy, the next that he is never lazy. Here he at first has nothing but praise for his Chevrolet, then shortly afterwards wonders why they let such cars be assembled at all. Again within a single speech he says that he is well liked and that others do not approve of him. Since he does seem to change so quickly, it may well be that his rapid transitions from hopefulness to despair are characteristic of his temperament.

As for the affair with the woman, he is not dissatisfied with Linda and does not seem proud of himself for having been unfaithful. He can usually find excuses for his actions, and here he mentally attributes his lapse to loneliness. Later he will give Biff the same reason. Yet when he is shown with the woman, he seems obviously to be enjoying himself. He relishes her flattering compliments and likes having his rather unsubtle jokes appreciated. Like Happy's conquests, the affair gives him the feeling of being a suave, irresistible man of the world. He cannot meet all the bills at home, but in Boston he can proffer a princely gift of stockings. In addition, the affair is good business, for the woman may give him entrée to see more buyers.

LINDA. The younger, more sparkling Linda is as kind to Willy as her older self. She tells him encouragingly that his future sales will be better and makes the current ones sound as good as possible. She assures him that he is good-looking and commends his lively talk. Yet, however soothing her words, she is never unaware of the harsh economic facts. She knows exactly, dollar for dollar, what things cost and what Willy brings in. And when Willy talks grandly of selling thousands, her quick, instinctive query is, "Did you sell anything?" Intent upon figuring the commission so that she can pay off bills, she forces him into embarrassing admissions of failure. But she recovers quickly and works to restore his confidence. Some critics, incidentally, have suggested that had the faithful Linda been more direct and less soothing, she might have helped Willy act more maturely.

BIFF. Right before the big game, Biff is seen as the idol of the neighborhood boys. They wait around in the Loman cellar and gladly execute his orders to sweep the furnace room or hang up the wash. Both Biff and his brother are good-natured about helping out at home. They gaily agree to take over the chores from Linda.

PLOT DEVELOPMENT. This is one more pleasant memory of family happiness and cooperation, which makes more disturbing the current tensions with Biff. In addition, it recalls Biff's moment of glory as the leader among the boys, as against the present status of Biff as an insignificant drifter. At the same time, the scene has its darker side. Willy is remembering that even in his prime, he was never much of a success. And he is haunted by the Boston affair that made him feel guilty about his disloyalty to Linda and that led to his troubles with Biff. There are thus in this scene various elements that help to increase the failing Willy's current anxieties.

TECHNIQUE.   The handling of this scene is somewhat unusual. The episode is a remembered one and is handled as a flashback. Within this memory, however, there is an additional one. Willy at present is recalling his past conversation with Linda. At the time, however, that he had that talk, he was reminded of a previous encounter with the woman in Boston. Special musical effects and a further use of lighting and scrim make the necessary distinctions onstage.

IMPORTANT THEMES. IMPORTANCE OF BEING WELL LIKED.   Willy is delighted here because Biff clearly is popular with the boys, who regard him as their leader. Willy sees here the proof of his theory as to what is the best qualification for success. As for himself, when he is worried about his own lack of progress, he is afraid that he is not well-enough liked.

FAMILY SOLIDARITY.   The boys gladly help out with the wash or get the furnace room swept. Linda and Willy talk of paying off household bills. Willy, seeing Linda and appreciating her love, is distressed to remember his disloyalty.

THE HARD STRUGGLE OF THE AVERAGE FAMILY.   There is much detailed reference here to nagging bills for car, roof, and household appliances. And Willy talks of the long hours of work necessary to make even fair commissions. *Death of a Salesman* is sometimes described as a tragedy of the "little man" or the "common man." Here the modest sums needed, that are so difficult for this family to raise, point up the low-income status of this man with the grand visions.

QUESTIONABLE MORALITY.   Both Happy and Biff have been seen earlier as unmarried men who have had affairs with women. Their ideal, however, has been a stable marriage with a good, steady girl like Linda. Willy hitherto has been the hero of his sons as good husband and good father. Here, however, he is shown to be guilty of marital infidelity. His excuse is—loneliness. But again, as before, the audience is made aware that Willy's moral standards can be curiously flexible.

SYMBOLS: THE WASH.   Linda, with her apron, her hair ribbon, and her basket of wash, is the housewife. Later, in Miller's play *After the Fall*, the first wife, Louise, also a woman whose main interest is the home, will usually be shown wearing an apron. Linda, with the wash, here is contrasted with the "other woman" in the hotel room.

STOCKINGS. Here the Boston woman thanks Willy for a gift of stockings. They represent Willy's attempt at cutting an impressive figure outside the home. Linda, it will be shown shortly, darns her own stockings. Given the economic straits of the Loman home, new stockings are a luxury.

ACT I, SCENE 6

SUMMARY. Watching Linda darn her stockings, in the continued memory episode, Willy angrily tells her to dispose of them. Bernard comes in with a new warning about Biff's failing. Willy also hears that Biff is being too forward with girls and is driving without a license. Willy does not want a spineless nonentity like Bernard, who will not cheat for Biff on final exams. But neither can he understand where Biff has obtained some of his dubious values.

CHARACTER ANALYSES

WILLY. Willy here is seen greatly disturbed by references to Biff's youthful wildness. Essentially Willy does not want Biff to steal or cheat or act in an ungentlemanly manner. He threatens even to beat him to make him stop. Yet Willy, Biff's idol, did describe his taking of the football as "initiative." And even now Willy is pleading with Bernard to give Biff answers on the final statewide Regents examinations. So there is irony in Willy's wondering where Biff could have learned such wrong ideas. His father always gave him "decent" standards.

BIFF. Despite the warnings Biff has not been studying. Instead he is driving without a license and being rough with the girls. Also he has not returned the football. The only explanation for such behavior is Bernard's report that a teacher considers Biff "stuck up." Willy has long been praising Biff and encouraging him to think well of himself. Biff has apparently become a very confident youth, certain that he can breeze through life doing what he pleases.

BERNARD. Bernard is anxious about Biff and willing to help him before the test. He refuses, however, to run the risk of being caught on an important final examination. Bernard, apparently, is not altogether above some dishonesty on behalf of a friend. He has, in the past, given Biff some answers. But Bernard is not one to jeopardize his whole future, either. So he refuses Willy's plea and is angrily silenced by the irate salesman. For all his helpfulness, incidentally, Bernard is always quoting school gossip and generally sounds a trifle smug.

PLOT DEVELOPMENT. Here Willy's shining confidence in Biff is put to the test, and Willy characteristically tries to make excuses and even deny the manifest truth. These memories, however, are distressing ones. Biff is riding for a fall, and his school difficulties will eventually lead to the break between him and Willy. The memory of this break and the events leading up to it weigh heavily upon the older Willy's confused mind.

TECHNIQUE.   This is largely straight flashback, without the overlapping effect of the previous scene. The only variation occurs when the Boston woman's laugh is heard half-mockingly amidst Willy's angry attempts to silence Biff's accusers. Willy seems particularly upset about Biff's rough behavior toward girls. Does the woman's laugh constitute a reminder of his own unauthorized romance? Or does it look ahead to the crucial break with Biff that will occur when Willy is discovered with her in compromising circumstances?

IMPORTANT THEMES: IMPORTANCE OF BEING WELL LIKED.   Even when Willy is alarmed about Biff's behavior, he still retorts that Biff has "spirit" and personality, in contrast to insignificant types like Bernard.

QUESTIONABLE MORALITY.   Willy threatens to punish Biff for stealing and misbehaving with the girls. But Willy also urges Bernard to give Biff answers dishonestly on the final examination.

FATHER-SON SOLIDARITY.   Even though he does not appear to be at all certain that Biff has acted admirably, Willy rudely silences Linda and angrily sends Bernard home.

SYMBOLS: THE FOOTBALL.   This is mentioned again, pointing up Biff's tendency to steal. Linda says that it should be returned. Willy furiously denies that this was stealing at all. After all, Biff is bringing it back.

THE STOCKINGS.   Willy irately demands that Linda throw away the stockings she is darning. Seeing her mending them makes him feel like a poor provider. He also has a sense of guilt, since he gave a box of stockings to the Boston woman. Characteristically, Willy mainly does not want to *see* Linda darning. Both he and Biff prefer to evade unpleasant reminders. Yet the memory scenes indicate that even when he can have disturbing matters removed from view, Willy can not get them out of his mind.

ACT I, SCENE 7

SUMMARY.   Back in the present, Happy comes down to coax Willy to bed. Willy laments that he never went to Alaska with his determined brother Ben and sneers at Happy's offer to finance his retirement. He is then visited by Charley, his quiet, compassionate neighbor. They play cards, and Willy scorns his friend as ignorant about vitamins and carpentry. He also proudly turns down his offer of a job. Willy then seems to see the long-dead adventurous Ben. He talks confusedly with both his vision and the bewildered Charley. Soon he insults the latter once more, and Charley resignedly goes home.

CHARACTER ANALYSES

WILLY.   Apparently much disturbed by the previous recollections, Willy acts irritably toward both Happy and Charley. He ridicules Happy's fine-sounding offer to "retire him for life." He knows how much his son makes and how much he spends on car, apartment, and women. Willy is not usually one to face facts squarely. But he recognizes here that his "woods are burning," and that there is small comfort in Happy's soothing assurances.

As for the affronts to Charley, there are three possible explanations. First of all, Willy is edgy with everybody. In the first scene he was irked because Linda bought a new type of cheese. Secondly, despite his kindliness, Charley always aggravates Willy's sense of failure. Charley has a good, flourishing business and a successful son. Finally, Willy keeps trying to see himself and his sons as superior beings. Charley could never put up a ceiling, but Willy is good with his hands. He finally angers even the unexcitable Charley by his rash statement that being unable to handle tools, Charley is not much of a man. But this hostile remark is in line with Willy's over-all stress upon those skills that he and his sons can claim to possess.

This scene also brings out Willy's admiration for his older brother Ben, who made a fortune in the jungle when he was young. To Willy, Ben stands for success through vision and determination. Ben knew what he wanted, went after it, and got it. He knew how to take advantage of opportunities in Alaska and Africa. Willy should have gone with him, for then he, too, would be rich. Both men represent the American dream of rising by one's own efforts from poverty and obscurity to great wealth. Ben, however, makes the daring move and realizes the ambition. Willy stays with the same small job, bragging about the past and making great predictions about the future. Ben is dream plus action; Willy is merely dream.

CHARLEY.   Charley is seen here as the amiable, understanding neighbor who sees that Willy is distraught and wants to calm him down. He comes to play cards with him in the dead of night in the hope of making him tired enough to sleep. He offers him a job on the chance that having an assured income would make him less irascible. He also takes considerable abuse from the short-tempered, uneasy Willy. Yet Charley does not lack spirit. He answers Willy quite sharply when the latter suggests that his inability to handle tools makes him less of a man. Indeed, Charley's suddenly authoritative tone reminds Willy of the brisk, assertive manner of his determined brother, Ben.

Just as Charley's son, Bernard, contrasts with Biff, so Charley is often seen in opposition to Willy. Charley is unassuming and unpretentious, but generally well adjusted and relatively successful. Over the years Charley's family has lived next door. The two homes, and hence the general economic background, are presumably similar. Charley, however, has not demanded as much from life as Willy, and, paradoxically, has apparently received more.

Charley and Willy are also contrasted as fathers. Here Willy confides in his friend that he is distressed about Biff's plan to return West. Willy is particularly saddened to think that he, being short of money, cannot give Biff anything. Charley, in general, feels that a thirty-four-year old son should be left to shift for himself. He urges Willy to let Biff go and "forget him." But Willy cannot do this, for his whole life is centered in his son. Later Charley and Bernard will visit on easy, friendly terms, man to man. By letting his son go, Charley keeps his pleasant relationship. Willy holds on, at least in his mind, and makes Biff and himself miserable.

HAPPY.   Happy is another who tries to calm Willy. Always one to gloss over unpleasantness, he attempts to halt Willy's regrets about the past and to assure Charley that nothing is wrong. He is interested, however, almost in spite of himself, in the legend of get-rich-quick Uncle Ben. Happy, like his father, dreams of making some impressive coup. But when, momentarily carried away with the vision, he assures Willy that he will finance his retirement, Willy snorts. He may not be able to recognize his own meaningless boasts, but he can puncture Happy's. So again Happy is shown to be the less favored son.

BEN.   Since Ben is seen only as one of Willy's disturbing memories, it is hard to know how far the vision represents a real person. Willy does tell Charley that his brother died recently in Africa and left seven sons. But Ben, as he appears from Willy's recollections, is a curious figure. Always hurrying off, after perfunctory questions about the family, he stands for two concepts. He is, first of all, rejected opportunity. Had Willy gone with him to Alaska, Willy would today have possessed a great fortune. Second, he is the cold, ruthless, triumphant victor over life's jungle. Ben knows what he wants, and lets nothing interfere. He is daring and unscrupulous in a way Willy could never be. There may well, of course, have been such a person. But some critics at least have wondered whether or not "Ben" was essentially a personification summing up certain of Willy's aspirations. He may well be the wild, adventurous pioneer that the more domesticated salesman at times wishes he could have been.

PLOT DEVELOPMENT. Here it becomes evident that Willy's crack-up cannot be kept within the family. Charley can hear his noisy, rambling talk from next door. And Charley also hears him talk confusedly to an unseen Ben. Another interesting development is Charley's offer of a job. Whatever is disturbing Willy, the solution cannot be found in mere economic security. Pride, of course, enters into his angry rejection of Charley's offer. But this only indicates further that Willy's sad decline is essentially a matter of inner tensions and anxieties.

TECHNIQUE. In this scene there is an even more startling use of combined objective events and Willy's mental figments. Willy at one time is conversing both with the actually present Charley and his vision of the now dead Ben. As a stage effect this is striking. There is some humor here as Charley tries to make sense out of this strange triangular parley. But it also serves to point up Willy's deteriorating condition.

IMPORTANT THEMES: SUCCESS THROUGH DARING VENTURES. Ben went into the jungle as a young man and came out with a fortune in diamonds. He never had to "grub for money." Willy regrets he never went off with Ben to Alaska for a similar rapidly acquired windfall.

FATHER-SON SOLIDARITY. Charley urges Willy to let Biff go and not worry about him further. Willy cannot do this. He wishes only that he had more to give Biff.

IMPORTANCE OF PHYSICAL PROWESS. Willy sneers bitterly at Charley for the latter cannot handle tools. Their manual skills always make the Loman men feel superior.

SYMBOLS: DIAMONDS. Ben's African cache of diamonds always represents to Willy the wealth to be obtained by vision and determination.

CEILING. Like the hammock, the overhanging bough, and the roof, the newly installed ceiling is used to emphasize Willy's skill with his hands, a type of work of which the more financially successful Charley is totally incapable. Throughout there is the suggestion that the Lomans have certain aptitudes that cannot be used remuneratively in the urban job area where they seek success.

ACT I, SCENE 8

SUMMARY.   Alone again, Willy relives Ben's one visit to Brooklyn. Ben and their father had gone off separately when Willy was a baby in South Dakota. Their father, says Ben, was a bold, adventurous man, who toured the land selling handmade flutes. Ben alarms Linda by urging Biff never to fight fairly with strangers. But Willy calls him a great man. To fix the stoop, Willy sends Biff to steal sand from the apartment builders. They have already taken lumber. Charley and Bernard, entering, decry this thievery but are ridiculed. As Ben leaves, he again tells Willy's sons how he made a fast fortune. He also reassures Willy that he is bringing his boys up well.

CHARACTER ANALYSES

WILLY.   This scene emphasizes anew Willy's strong family feelings. He welcomes Ben and wants to hear more of their father. He is also eager to show how well he works with his boys by repairing the stoop while Ben waits. Again Willy shows his contempt for Charley and Bernard because they cannot work so well with their hands. And again he reveals dubious moral values by encouraging Biff's stealing. At the same time, his anxious questions to Ben as to how well he is educating his sons show the anxiety and uncertainty that plagued even the younger, more assured Willy.

BEN.   Ben has a courtly graciousness as he greets Linda, but he can also be frightening. As he shows Biff how to fight, he trips him and poises his umbrella point over the boy's eye. He also is not disturbed about the stolen lumber. His sense of family responsibility also seems never to have been very strong. It appears that when he left the wagon in South Dakota as a lad of seventeen, he walked off from his mother and the very young Willy, the father having already deserted them to head for Alaska. This is his one visit to Willy, and he has to ask if their mother is still alive. Ben, however, is completely sure of himself and proud of his quickly acquired fortune in diamonds. He has never kept books, and some of his enterprises may have been questionable. But to the uncertain, struggling Willy he exudes success, and is therefore a "great man."

LINDA.   Linda is not favorably impressed. She does not like Ben's insisting that Biff practice fighting. And she is horrified when ,he trips the boy, menaces him with the tip of his umbrella, and warns him against fighting too fairly with strangers. Linda is also worried when Biff is chased by the watchman after stealing some sand. In general, Linda's standards seem somewhat higher than Willy's. But her protests tend to be mild. Her "Biff, dear!" as she runs off, alarmed, does not sound as if she were about to be sternly unforgiving.

CHARLEY. Looking somewhat absurd in knickers, Charley comes over to warn Willy about Biff's risk of being arrested. Charley is always the good neighbor, as is his son who comes to announce that Biff is being chased by the watchman. As usual, however, the well-meant, if officious, efforts of both are scornfully repulsed. Again, too, the point is made that neither can hammer nails.

BIFF. Again the young Biff is shown eager to obey his father and to work with him on the stoop. He also is not at all annoyed that Willy should ask him to steal. He and Happy are said by Willy to be "fearless characters," with Biff possessing "nerves of iron." Such praise seems to be encouraging them to have little respect for the property rights of others.

PLOT DEVELOPMENT. Willy's memories of Ben and Ben's impressively rapid acquisition of enormous wealth will later be influential in Willy's debate with himself about committing suicide for the insurance money. Also Biff's stealing, with parental encouragement, will help to make the later Oliver episode more catastrophic.

TECHNIQUE. This is a straight flashback scene with no interweaving of action in the present.

IMPORTANT THEMES: FAMILY SOLIDARITY. Willy admires his brother and wants to hear more of their father, whom Ben describes with enthusiasm. Willy is proud of his sons as "rugged, well liked, and fearless." Ben praises Willy as a good father to his "manly" sons.

QUESTIONABLE MORALITY. Willy encourages the boys to steal sand and lumber from the construction company. He does not protest when Ben encourages Biff to fight unfairly.

IMPORTANCE OF PHYSICAL PROWESS. Willy is eager to show how he and the boys can fix the stoop. He also claims that Biff can cut down a tree. He sneers at the neighbors who cannot hammer nails.

IMPORTANCE OF BEING WELL LIKED. Willy tells Ben that he is bringing his boys up to be popular. Ben approves of his training.

SUCCESS THROUGH DARING VENTURES. Willy holds Ben up to the boys as a great man because he made a fast fortune in the jungle. Ben praises his father because through gadgets he made more money in one week than Willy could all his life. This is undoubtedly nonsense, but Biff has said that he was never brought up to "grub for money." And Ben seems again to be stressing the quick return.

SYMBOLS: THE WASH. The younger Linda, entering with the wash, seems to personify the settled domestic life as against Ben's invitation to adventurous doings in far-off lands. Linda is hostile to Ben.

THE STOOP. This repair job of Willy's will be mentioned fondly by Biff after his father's death. It represents his expert manual skills and his interest in the home. It is also his limited answer to Ben. If he has not found a fortune in diamonds, he can at least fix a stoop. Yet even this irreproachable activity is tied in with Biff's stealing and with mean sneers at the less handy neighbors.

DIAMONDS. Again these represent the quick, fabulous fortune.

KNICKERS. Charley wears knickers that his wife picked out for him. Here the outfit contrasts Charley as a hen-pecked little man who cannot work with his hands with the more assertive Loman men who have such skills. Charley and Bernard are worried about the thefts and are clearly not "fearless characters." The contrast between the families is always somewhat ironic, but here the knickers give Willy one more chance to voice ridicule and contempt.

THE WATCH. Ben, in Willy's visions, is always looking at his watch and hurrying off. Never, apparently, having seen much of father or brother, Willy is always pleading for more help, and never getting more than a few terse statements. Ben is an elusive memory. In a sense, too, the watch seems to point up the need for quick decisions when an opportunity presents itself. Willy thinks of himself as having had only one brief chance to reach for untold wealth. He missed it. He will later see a second such chance in the suicide plan.

ACT I, SCENE 9

SUMMARY. The vision of Ben fades, and Willy is rejoined by Linda, who reminds him that they long ago pawned Ben's diamond watch-fob gift for Biff's correspondence courses. Willy then, in slippers, goes out for a walk. The boys come down, and Linda says that Willy is worse when Biff returns. Biff promises to reform. Linda speaks lovingly of Willy. He is old and worn but deserves respect. Despite his long service, the company has put him back on straight commission, and so he secretly borrows from Charley. His sons are neglectful. She adds that Willy plans suicide. Once he smashed the car, and he still hides a rubber tube for inhaling gas. The boys are horrified. Biff will again tackle the business world, but thinks all three would be better off as carpenters working in the open air.

CHARACTER ANALYSES

WILLY. This scene emphasizes Willy's disturbed personality. He insists upon going out late at night in his slippers. And, more alarmingly, he has actually tried suicide. Linda also points out that he has been a good, hard-working man deserving of some consideration. She also stresses his continued concern for his undeserving sons.

LINDA. Linda speaks affectionately and admiringly of Willy but she is not completely blind as to his limitations. She has to admit that he is not easy to live with. She knows that he deceives her about the gas device. She admits that he is not a "great man" or even the "finest character." If she is to this extent clearsighted about Willy, she is even more harsh as regards the boys. She chides them for their neglect, tells Biff to treat his father more respectfully, and speaks scornfully of Happy as a "philandering bum." She condemns both as ungrateful, and will not permit them to sympathize with her if it means attacking Willy. She may patiently soothe and encourage Willy, but to the boys she can be spirited, sharp, and uncompromising. Either Biff behaves himself or he leaves the house.

BIFF. In this scene Biff is seen to be confused and upset. He is fond of his mother and eager to please her. At the same time he obviously has some grudge against Willy, whom she so staunchly defends. He feels guilty when Linda tells him that his coming causes Willy to become more agitated. Yet if Willy needs help, Biff must stay around and get a job. He obviously hates the business world and feels ill at ease about trying to reenter it. Yet as Linda talks of Willy's misfortunes and his need for help, Biff feels miserable and promises to help. Throughout he appears to be goodhearted but very uncertain as to his course.

HAPPY.   As usual, Happy tries ineffectually to make everything seem all right. He tries to reassure Linda that Biff really is devoted to Willy. He also claims, in opposition to Biff, that Willy has treated Linda with consideration. And he is sure that the insurance company was wrong in suggesting that Willy's car crashes were intentional. When, however, Biff turns on him, he answers angrily, defending Willy against his brother. Yet even he is disgusted when he learns of Willy's concealment of the gas-inhaling tube.

PLOT DEVELOPMENT.   The story told by Linda of Willy's desperate plight motivates Biff more strongly to try to get a loan from Oliver. The references to the suicide attempts help to prepare for the final self-destructive course determined upon by Willy.

TECHNIQUE.   Except for the scene in the boys' bedroom, this is the first in which Willy is not present. The central role is a demanding one, for Willy is on the stage most of the time. Many of the scenes in which he figures involve memories that may or may not be distorted. A scene like this, however, with only Linda and the boys is usually considered to be more objective. This, of course, takes place in the present, and no flashbacks are involved.

IMPORTANT THEMES: CORRUPTION IN MODERN BUSINESS.   Willy has worked for almost thirty-six years for the company. During that time he has opened up new markets and served them faithfully. The company, however, shows no gratitude. As his production slows up with increasing age, he is deprived of a steady salary and put back on straight commission like a beginner. The treatment, as Linda sees it, is inhuman and plays havoc with a man's self-respect. Linda also notes the lack of the personal element in business now. In the past old friends used to help Willy with an occasional extra order. Now he is neither known nor welcomed.

Finally, Biff admits that he has never liked the business world. Happy says that is because he never tried to please people and because he has acted irresponsibly. Biff, it seems, used to whistle in elevators. He also took days off to go swimming, but without playing Happy's game of having others lie for him. So here there are objections to the regimentation and routine of the business world, although it must be conceded that Biff and Happy are not altogether reliable critics. Both are somewhat immature in their attitudes.

FAMILY SOLIDARITY.   Linda strongly affirms her love for Willy and all but demands that the two sons help him. Otherwise they are as "ungrateful" as the company. Happy's fifty-dollar Christmas gift is scornfully judged to be insufficient. The boys accept Linda's view, and Biff promises to get a job and give his father half his paycheck.

QUESTIONABLE MORALITY. Happy claims that Biff used to take time off for swimming and thus failed to make a good impression on employers. Happy's system is to go off when he pleases but to have others lie about his whereabouts.

COUNTRY VERSUS CITY. When working in the city, Biff could not whistle in an elevator without being thought mad. Biff wishes that he, his father, and his brother could work as carpenters out on the open prairie. Then they would be free from the "nuthouse" city and free to whistle. As devotees of the outdoor life, both brothers, apparently, have skipped work on summer days to go swimming.

FATHER-SON CONFLICT. Biff is saddened to learn of Willy's plight but still harbors some deep personal resentment. His pledge to help Willy comes half from a sense of duty and half from a desire to please the adamant Linda.

SYMBOLS: DIAMOND WATCH FOB. Ben's prized gift of a diamond watch fob went to pay for Biff's courses. Willy will later think a great deal of Ben and diamonds when he plans another grand gesture to save Biff.

THE CAR. Willy's car, hitherto a means of earning his livelihood, is now seen as a possible suicide device, and it will later be used as such.

THE RUBBER TUBE. This also signifies Willy's urge toward self-destruction. But Linda's respect for Willy will not let her destroy it.

ACT I, SCENE 10

SUMMARY. Willy returns, angered to hear Biff reduce them to carpenters. He sneers at Biff until he hears of the scheme to borrow money from Oliver. Then with enthusiasm he gives much contradictory advice. Happy says that the Loman Brothers, as a team, could sell sporting goods. Excited over the idea, Willy is rude to Linda, thus infuriating Biff. Yet Biff agrees to soothe him, before going up to bed. Biff is suddenly confident about the future.

CHARACTER ANALYSES

WILLY. In this scene, Willy is rude and unreasonable. He is angry and possibly frightened because Biff has said that people laugh at Willy. So he must reassert himself as the "big shot" and set Biff down. He is also either muddled in his thinking or, as before, very changeable. He tells Biff one moment to act dignified and reserved with Oliver, the next to start the interview with some lively stories.

When he hears about the Oliver plan and also Happy's idea of the Loman Brothers business, he is immediately hopeful and enthusiastic. Yet his very optimism and feverish excitement make him even more rude and arrogant, and so the battle flares up anew.

BIFF.   Although driven to defend himself, Biff tries to be patient, largely, in all probability, for Linda's sake. Only when Willy harshly silences his wife does Biff completely lose his temper. In this scene, however, there is also the old assured Biff. However slim are his actual chances with Oliver, Biff, like his father and brother, has sudden high hopes.

LINDA.   At this point Linda is essentially a buffer, or peacemaker between father and son.

HAPPY.   The younger son, too, tries to quell the hot tempers of Willy and Biff. He also here reveals a creative idea of his own. The brothers will team up to demonstrate and sell sports equipment. Like other Loman schemes this is not altogether practicable in view of their lack of standing and lack of material resources. But as an idea it does show a certain flair. As eager as the other two, Happy says that such a partnership would permit a friendly arrangement based upon mutual trust, not cutthroat competition. And they could also take time off to go swimming. There is something brash and boyish about Happy's vision, but then all the Loman men are to some extent immature.

PLOT DEVELOPMENT.   This scene raises the hopes of all, despite the personal clashes, and sends Biff off with assurance to call on Oliver. The failure of the project will plunge Willy more deeply into despair.

TECHNIQUE.   There are no flashbacks here. This seems to be straight present-day action. It is a strong scene dramatically because of the intense conflicts.

IMPORTANT THEMES: FAMILY SOLIDARITY: Happy wants to work with Biff and will help him prepare for the interview. Happy and Linda try to keep peace in the family. Willy, in more tractable moments, tries to give Biff helpful advice and encouragement.

FATHER-SON CONFLICT: Willy resents what he considers Biff's contempt for him as being laughable. Willy also objects to Biff's rough talk, and Biff in turn all but accuses his father of hypocrisy. Biff also takes Linda's part when Willy shouts at her.

CORRUPTION OF MODERN BUSINESS.   Happy would like to have Biff as his business partner. For then there would be "honor" and those friendly ties missing in the business world as Happy knows it. They would also have more personal freedom, for example, to go swimming, without always being afraid that someone else would take advantage of them.

ACT I, SCENE 11

SUMMARY.   Upstairs, preparing for bed, Willy complains about the defective shower. But his hopes for Biff now are high. Both sons come to bid him good night, and he again loads Biff with dubious advice. He thinks of Biff at his moment of greatness when the fans cheered at Ebbets field. Linda soothes him with a lullaby, and he agrees to see Howard in the morning and ask for a New York assignment. Meanwhile, Biff, smoking downstairs, finds and removes the rubber tubing Willy hides away as a suicide device.

CHARACTER ANALYSES

WILLY.   Willy continues in a highly excitable condition. He also has the optimistic notion that Biff's football success will be matched when he sees Oliver. After all, Biff has a greatness about him. Ironically, he warns Biff not to act subservient, but that is just how he himself will act with Howard, his boss.

BIFF.   Troubled about Willy and yet desirous of pleasing Linda, Biff comes to say good night. Again Willy irritates him, but he controls his anger. Later he is appalled to find the rubber tubing.

LINDA.   Again Linda acts with almost maternal solicitude for Willy, even singing him a lullaby. She also, however, takes advantage of his hopefulness about Biff to urge him to go to see Howard. All through this and the last scene, she patiently accepts Willy's rudeness with remarkably good grace.

HAPPY.   Biff being noticeably quiet, Happy tries to make noise enough to prevent another outbreak. He also assures Linda that he is getting married. This seems a bid for attention, much like his earlier claims to Willy that he was losing weight. And it elicits the same very limited notice.

PLOT DEVELOPMENT.   Linda seizes the moment of Willy's optimism regarding Biff to press him to approach Howard for an easier job. Willy listens to her and agrees to go the following morning. This crucial interview on the same day as Biff's attempt to see Oliver will accelerate Willy's downfall. In addition, Biff's finding of the tubing will intensify the young man's anxiety and strain, thus making his failure to convince Oliver seem the more devastating to him.

TECHNIQUE. Although there is no flashback here in the usual sense, an interesting effect is secured with lights. As Willy recalls Biff's day of triumph on the football field, he compares him to the Greek god Hercules, known for his strength. Linda, in turn, remembers his gold uniform. Meanwhile Biff stands on the lower stage level, outside the house, smoking. A gold light is then played upon him, and the audience sees him looking very much like Willy's bright image of his son at an earlier age. Lighting is also used to call attention to the gas heater, behind which Biff finds the length of tubing.

IMPORTANT THEMES: IMPORTANCE OF PHYSICAL PROW-ESS. Biff, to Willy, must have greatness in him because he was an outstanding football player.

FAMILY SOLIDARITY. The boys come in to bid Willy good night in hopes of soothing him and reestablishing general harmony.

FATHER-SON CONFLICT. Biff remains quiet, but he is obviously irked by his father's excited counsel.

QUESTIONABLE MORALITY. Willy urges Biff to lie to Oliver about his experience out West.

SYMBOL: THE RUBBER TUBE. Linda knows about the tubing, but will not remove it lest she hurt Willy's pride. Biff, however, is not so sensitive on this score. In hopes of staving off such a disaster, he takes the tubing away. Later, however, in the midst of a furious battle with his father, he will refer to it as a symbol of his father's weakness.

ACT II, SCENE I

SUMMARY. The next morning Willy, rested and hopeful, breakfasts with Linda. He talks of a house in the country and of building guest houses. Linda asks him to get a two-hundred-dollar advance from Howard. This will pay off their house after twenty-five years. She then tells him Biff and Happy have invited him to dinner that night. He leaves in high spirits. Biff calls, and Linda encourages him and tells him to be kind to Willy.

CHARACTER ANALYSES

WILLY. Willy here hits his final peak of confidence. Buoyed up by the boys' hopes, as well as his own, he is sure that he can persuade Howard. He is somewhat discouraged to hear how much they owe. By the time they pay off refrigerator and car, both are worn out. But he shares Linda's satisfaction in at last, after a quarter of a century, making a final payment on the house. Again, too, in this scene there is the Willy who enjoys working with his hands. He talks with pride of the repairs he has made in the house, and he looks forward to building guest houses for his sons when they move to a home in the country. Finally, his deep affection for the boys is evident. He is overjoyed that they have invited him to dinner.

LINDA. In this scene Linda is her usual encouraging self, but even she seems more than usually optimistic, caught up apparently in the mood of her husband and sons. As before, she has no illusions about their needs. In nudging Willy again to see Howard, she reels off the exact amounts that they require for insurance, car repair, refrigerator, and mortgage payments. Yet in view of what she knows about the company that put the aging Willy back on straight commission, she seems remarkably naive in urging him to ask for a two-hundred-dollar advance. At this point she sounds like Biff setting out to ask for ten to fifteen thousand dollars from a man he once robbed. Her deep love for Willy, however, is also evident throughout and especially during the telephone conversation with Biff. She tells him to greet his father affectionately, for Willy is "only a little boat looking for a harbor."

PLOT DEVELOPMENT. The optimistic mood here sends the hitherto beaten and despairing Willy off to make demands upon Howard. At the same time, in view of Linda's outlining of heavy debts, it is clear that this is a last desperate chance for Willy, as is the Oliver scheme for Biff. Hence if the plea is refused, as it well may be, the consequences are likely to be grave.

TECHNIQUE. This is straight present-day conversation between Willy and Linda, but sprightly, hopeful background music is used to emphasize the mood of early-morning optimism.

IMPORTANT THEMES: COUNTRY VERSUS CITY. Willy looks forward to a house in the country where he can grow things again. He also wants to build a guest house or two there. They can raise chickens and have a vegetable garden. This would be the good life.

THE HARD STRUGGLE OF THE AVERAGE FAMILY. Much is made here of the painfully slow business of paying on the installment plan for household appliances and the car and keeping every-thing in repair. Insurance premiums must be met before the grace period expires, and mortgage payments must be met over a quarter of a century. Willy has never been the illustrious figure he some-times tries to picture himself, but he has until recently met his obligations.

FAMILY SOLIDARITY.   Linda encourages both Willy and Biff. Willy expresses high hopes for Biff. The boys want to entertain their father at dinner.

SYMBOLS: THE STOCKINGS.   Willy sees Linda about to darn stockings and asks her not to do so while he is around. The fact that he gave stockings to the Boston woman will be brought up again significantly in a future scene.

THE RUBBER TUBING.   Discovering it missing from its usual place, Linda has hopefully concluded that Willy has given up the idea of suicide. She is, therefore, somewhat deflated to hear that Biff has taken it.

SEEDS.   Willy talks often of happier days when there was more light and air and they could grow flowers and vegetables. Now, feeling hopeful, he plans to buy seeds to try again. Whether it be through plants or sons, Willy wants a sense of starting something that will develop fully in the future. His one regret about the house, now practically paid for, is that strangers will take it over after he and Linda can no longer occupy it.

ACT II, SCENE 2

SUMMARY.   At the office Willy is virtually ignored by Howard, who plays fascinatedly with an expensive new tape recorder. Willy, bluffing, says he will get one too. Reminding Howard of a Christ-mas party pledge of an office job, he vainly requests sixty-five or even fifty dollars a week. Coldly refused, he talks glowingly of the good old days, when Dave Singleton, aged eighty-four, could still take orders by phone since business was then on a friendly, man-to-man basis. Willy adds that Howard's father promised him advancement and decries Howard's failure to honor commitments. Impatiently, Howard leaves, and Willy panics when he accidental-ly turns on the recorder. Howard returns, and despite Willy's pleas to be allowed to go back to Boston, discharges him altogether.

CHARACTER ANALYSES

WILLY.   At first Willy is the foolish braggart, talking of buying a hundred-fifty-dollar machine when he needs more than that just to cover debts. Then, begging for smaller and smaller sums just to keep going, he seems a pitiable, broken old man. Gradually, however, his anger restores his dignity. Outraged by Howard's chill indifference, he cries, "You can't eat the orange and throw the peel away." And his demand to be treated as a human being is a moving one. His subsequent shouting recalls the disturbed Willy of earlier scenes, but his nostalgic references to his family and to old Dave Singleton give him a strong human appeal in opposition to the impersonal efficiency of Howard.

HOWARD. This impatient young executive is no conventional deep-dyed villain. As compared, for instance, with the sensual Happy, he is the solid, respectable husband and father. He enjoys listening to his small son's voice on the new tape recorder, and he thinks of using the gadget to make sure that he does not miss the Jack Benny program, a comedy show. Yet to Howard, "business is business." He will talk pleasantly enough to employees. But if they do not bring in profits, they are expendable. He has no interest whatsoever in Willy's past record, his association with Wagner, Senior, or with pledges made years ago. Nor does he care how much Willy needs to feed his family. Willy's problems are his own affair. Howard's only concern is with the efficient operation of his firm. His total absorption in the tape recorder and his running off from the excited Willy suggest a shallow, rather immature man. But essentially he represents the cold, practical impersonality of modern business.

PLOT DEVELOPMENT. Although Willy's confidence was high upon leaving home and Linda, the opposition from the strictly mechanical tape recorder tends to unnerve him. He loses assurance rapidly, and even though his plea has a certain simple eloquence, he is clearly not going to be able to talk to Howard. This scene, therefore, leaves little doubt that Willy has lost his one chance. From now on, unless, of course, Biff accomplishes his improbable mission, Willy's progress will be unmistakably downhill.

TECHNIQUE. This scene in the present is interesting because of the effects secured by the tape recorder. It reveals Howard's intense personal concern with his own family and total lack of any such concern about Willy. It also works on Willy's nerves as it drones on and on. Finally, it somehow opposes the machine aspect of business dealings to the human, more personal element that Willy eulogizes.

IMPORTANT THEMES: CORRUPTION OF MODERN BUSINESS. Willy has worked for over thirty years for the Wagner Company. Even though "business is business," his plea for slightly more consideration as a human being would seem here to be justified.

LAMENT FOR THE PAST.   Willy remembers with pride the self-reliance and adventurous streak of his father and his brother. He also recalls the respect and friendship with which old Dave Singleton was treated as an aging salesman, and the warm association between himself and Howard's father.

SYMBOLS: THE TAPE RECORDER.   This associates Howard with a small-minded, gadget-ridden race of second-generation businessman. He obviously lacks the vision and basic generosity of his father. His pleasure is in the mechanical, and he has about him little of the humane.

DAVE SINGLETON.   Old Dave, eighty-four, taking orders by telephone from his hotel room while relaxing in his green velvet slippers, represents what Willy thought and hoped would be his reward for years of hard work selling. Actually, times have changed, and even in his sixties, Willy cannot make a living. One may ask whether this figure from the past is objectively recalled, or whether Willy has in his own mind raised Dave and perhaps brother Ben to a sort of heroic myth.

ACT II, SCENE 3

SUMMARY.   Seeing Ben again in his mind, Willy asks how he succeeded. He then recalls a past visit, in which Ben proposed that he go to Alaska. Linda, young again, carrying the wash, counters that Willy makes enough selling to be happy without. leaving. She talks of Wagner's promises and of old Dave. Ben is skeptical, but Willy points to young Biff, the football hero, with scholarship offers. Willy and Biff will get their "diamonds" through being well liked by business contacts. Ben leaves.

CHARACTER ANALYSES

WILLY.   Here Willy appears indecisive. He wants to take Ben's offer of work supervising Alaskan timberland. But he listens when Linda talks of his great future in selling. He is convinced that selling is his best choice because he sees Biff already on the road to success, entirely on the basis of being well liked. Of course, Willy here is unduly optimistic even about Biff, since the scholarship offers from the three universities are contingent upon Biff's passing all his subjects.

BEN.   As always, in a hurry, Ben talks of fighting for a fortune on the Alaskan frontier as opposed to the slow, discouraging progress made in cities. Cities have law courts, and Ben is not one to put up with hampering restrictions. He also likes the material satisfaction of owning property. He has no use for Willy's idea that building contacts will mean future security. Ben has vision, but he is also hard, practical, and ruthless.

LINDA.   Seen again with the wash, Linda defends her settled domestic domain against Ben's disturbing challenge to Willy. Linda dislikes Ben and all that he stands for. She talks of Willy's popularity and of his future with the firm. She recalls old Dave Singleton, always one of Willy's ideals. And she denies that one must conquer the world in order to attain true happiness. She fights for her home and she wins.

PLOT DEVELOPMENT.   Discharged by Howard, Willy is bitter and bewildered. Remembering the past when he turned down Ben's offer to settle for bright prospects in selling, he wonders whether he took the wrong course. More and more Ben's idea of the quick, decisive act, leading to a fabulous fortune, will appeal to him and help him decide to kill himself for the insurance money.

TECHNIQUE.   Willy's first question to Ben as to where he went wrong is based upon his heartsick reaction to the Howard interview. This, however, leads into a flashback scene in which Ben apparently gave Willy a chance to go to Alaska, shortly before Biff's great Senior game.

IMPORTANT THEMES: COUNTRY VERSUS CITY.   Willy would enjoy working with his sons out in the open in the Alaskan timberlands; there would be no installments to pay, and a man could make a fortune using his hands. Yet, prodded by Linda, Willy also finds the city challenging. Great wealth is there, too, if only those seeking it are well liked, presumably like Willy and Biff.

IMPORTANCE OF BEING WELL LIKED.   Linda says that Willy is well liked. As a result he will be happy and he will also get to be a partner in the firm. Willy picks up her argument. Great fortunes can be made if a man has good contacts who like him. The popular Biff has offers from universities and will be well received when he enters the business world.

SYMBOLS: THE WASH.   This homely manifestation of Linda's concern for her household identifies her with the settled life of an ordinary urban family. What this represents is diametrically opposed to the restless, opportunistic, adventurous life offered by Ben.

VALISE AND UMBRELLA. Ben is always anxiously on the move. He is always en route to make new deals and conquer new territories. He also, one suspects, may be leaving some dubious practice as far behind him as possible. He wants nothing to do with law courts, or the regulation they impose upon rugged individuals. The umbrella might seem strange equipment for such a fearless type. But he has been seen to use it as a weapon, aiming it at Biff's eye.

DAVE SINGLETON. Again the aging salesman is used to conjure up visions of a leisurely, profitable selling career, once the contacts have been firmly established.

DIAMONDS. Willy talks of diamonds being the reward of the successful salesman as well as the successful pioneer. Because of his admiration for Ben, Willy tends always to think of fortunes in terms of diamonds. He will later think of them when he is contemplating suicide. They are his symbol for riches.

ACT II, SCENE 4

SUMMARY. In this flashback scene, it is the day of Biff's big game. Bernard and Happy contend for the honor of carrying his helmet. If Biff wins, he will be captain of the championship city team. Charley teases Willy, who is feverishly enthusiastic, about never growing up. Willy, furious, blasts him for his ignorance.

CHARACTER ANALYSES

WILLY. Enormously proud of his football-hero son, Willy is boyishly eager to get to the field and wave his pennant. If this is Biff's greatest day, it is Willy's too. He is incredulous that Charley can be so stupid as to see it as only one more game and Willy as amusingly immature. Hot-tempered throughout his life, he wants to fight Charley but contents himself with name-calling. Although he sees the game as representing personal glory for Biff, as well as for his family, he also never loses sight of possible material rewards. Previously he has often mentioned the scholarship offers. Now he suggests that some professional team may pay Biff twenty-five thousand a year, the sum paid Red Grange.

BIFF. In his few speeches, Biff is first of all eager to get started. He is also the lordly but gracious idol, as he kindly permits Bernard to carry his shoulder guards. Finally, he is Willy's devoted son, again promising to make a special touchdown just for Dad.

HAPPY and BERNARD. Both here are Biff's satellites, vying to carry his helmet and shoulder guards and be seen with him in the clubhouse. Both are pleased just to be part of his retinue.

CHARLEY. On the whole a good, friendly neighbor, Charley here teases Willy unmercifully. Linda is probably right in her assertion that he is joking when he indicates that he did not know this was the day of the big game. But it is at least possible that his knowledge of football is limited. In any event, to him this is clearly only a boy's game, not worth all the fuss Willy makes over it. He is amusedly skeptical when Willy calls this the "greatest day" in Biff's life. Partly, then, Charley's jests stem from his own wry sense of humor, partly from the fact that his values differ markedly from Willy's.

PLOT DEVELOPMENT. Biff's sense of exaltation based on popularity and athletic prowess will be painfully lost when suddenly thereafter he is just one more student who failed a subject. And the consequences of his fall will eventually lead to Willy's self-destruction. In addition, Willy's memory of his denunciation of Charley's stupidity is one more disturbing thought as he now, penniless after losing his job, comes to seek a "loan" from the still amicable, reasonably successful Charley.

TECHNIQUE. For this flashback scene there is the bright, cheerful music of happier times. In addition, it may be noted that when Willy goes from kitchen to living room, he seemingly walks through a wall. This practice, followed in other scenes taking place now in Willy's mind, increases the effect of a sort of dream vision.

IMPORTANT THEMES: IMPORTANCE OF ATHLETIC PROWESS. Biff as champion will be cheered by thousands. His victory will mean that this is "the greatest day" of his life and may earn him a contract to be paid a great sum in professional football.

FAMILY SOLIDARITY. All the Lomans are off to the game, one to play, the other three to cheer. Biff, in turn, promises to make a special touchdown for his father.

ACT II, SCENE 5

SUMMARY. Having walked to Charley's office, back in the present, Willy alarms Jenny, the secretary, with his wild mumbling, then tries a feeble joke or two. He then meets Bernard, now a prosperous young lawyer off to plead a case in Washington. He takes tennis rackets to play on the courts of rich friends there. He is also married, and has two sons. Willy tries to bluff about Biff's success, but finally asks Bernard why Biff lost heart. Bernard cautiously suggests that Biff's collapse really occurred not after the school failure but following a subsequent visit to Willy in Boston. After that Biff fought Bernard and burned his prized sneakers. Disturbed by Bernard's hint that he was to blame, Willy turns on him furiously.

CHARACTER ANALYSES

WILLY. Several traits of Willy appear in this brief scene. First of all he is the disturbed personality, muttering something about touchdowns so that Jenny calls for help from Bernard. Then, getting hold of himself, he is again the genial salesman with a snappy quip for a pretty receptionist. Bernard's evident affluence much impresses him. To Willy material possessions are extremely significant. If Bernard's friends own tennis courts, they must be "fine people." And Bernard, having done so well, is no longer the anemic pest, but a "brilliant man." Willy as braggart is also here, for at first he tries almost pitiably to claim an equal success for Biff in the West. But soon he is again the forlorn, bewildered father, trying to understand. At the same time, he is not ready to accept any imputation of guilt, however blameworthy he actually feels. So once more his fiery temper flares.

BERNARD. Quietly assured, Bernard greets "Uncle Willy" pleasantly and asks about Biff. Generally tactful, he refrains from critical comments but tries to answer Willy's questions. In his account of Biff's erratic actions the summer after senior year, he reveals his love for Biff, despite the latter's having rarely treated him fairly. He does not know what happened in Boston but has realized that the incident there was crucial as far as Biff's later instability was concerned. Interestingly enough, however, the first explanation of Bernard, the student, was that Biff "never trained himself."

BIFF. From Bernard's account, the young Biff is shown to be highly emotional and given to dramatic gestures. The failure in school failed to daunt him particularly, but after some incident involving his father, he pummeled the inoffensive Bernard and burned his sneakers, with the University's name printed on them, as an indication that he had abandoned all his high hopes. Biff is also seen as someone who could inspire affection and loyalty even though he could be quite highhanded.

PLOT DEVELOPMENT. In this present-day scene, Bernard's obvious prosperity and settled home life with a wife and two sons make Willy even more painfully aware of Biff's unproductive existence. This adds to his desperation. In addition, Bernard's account of the past stirs up guilt feelings that he has been apparently trying to suppress. Soon, however, the Boston episode will be uppermost in his mind, and this agonizing memory also will serve to impel him toward destruction.

TECHNIQUE.   This scene is played on the front of the stage to the right. The office is suggested quite simply by a receptionist's small table. Bernard's suitcase and tennis rackets are props, and the lighting directs audience attention to this stage area.

IMPORTANT THEMES: "LOSTNESS."   Willy reveals to Bernard that he does not understand how so much could go wrong for Biff and begs for enlightenment.

FAMILY SOLIDARITY.   Willy wants still to help Biff, his one lament being that he has "nothing to give him."

QUESTIONABLE MORALITY.   Willy tries at first his usual lies, asserting that Biff is doing well out West and has actually been sent for by Oliver. Again, in talking of the teacher who failed Biff, Willy regards this action as evidence that the instructor was meanly responsible for ruining his son. For his part, while he talks of possibly having been at fault, Willy angrily denies being to blame once the idea has been broached by Bernard.

SYMBOLS: TENNIS RACKETS.   To Willy these suggest the good, leisured society to which the fortunate Bernard has access. Curiously enough, Bernard, either too puny for football or too engrossed in studies, now as a man participates in athletics.

THE SNEAKERS.   These shoes, as before, signify Biff's ambition to go on scholarship to the University. Burning them, he renounces his dream.

ACT 2, SCENE 6

SUMMARY.   Bernard leaves, with a bottle of bourbon, a gift from Charley. Bidding Willy goodbye, he suggests that Willy "walk away" from the insoluble problem. Willy cannot. Willy is further startled to learn that Bernard will plead before the Supreme Court, although his father never lavished much attention on him. Charley again offers Willy a job and is furiously repulsed. He tells Willy to grow up and stop thinking about being well liked. Giving Willy the money he needs, he accuses him of being jealous. Thinking of his insurance, Willy says he is worth more dead. He leaves dreamily, sending apologies to Bernard and touchingly taking leave of Charley as his one and only friend.

CHARACTER ANALYSES

WILLY. Here certain contradictions in Willy's nature become even more obvious. He can steadily borrow from Charley sizable sums that he may never be able to repay. Yet because he is allegedly keeping strict accounts, he feels that he is not accepting favors. If Charley objects, he will walk out haughtily. When, however, Charley offers him a job with no traveling, paying as much as he begged from Howard, he refuses with finality. At first he says that he does not need a job, then he simply says that he cannot work for his friend. Becoming an employee of the "big ignoramus" he has always scorned would be an insupportable humiliation, whereas he can still apparently convince himself that he will pay back the "loans." Willy is a proud man and as irascible as ever. Yet his last word to Charley indicates that deep within him there is some sense of gratitude.

CHARLEY. Proud of Bernard, Charley implies that he succeeded as a father because he did not smother his son with attention the way Willy did Biff. He now sends Bernard off to Washington with a friendly wave and a man-to-man gift of bourbon. Still spirited enough to fend off Willy's worst insults, Charley compassionately offers his old antagonist a job. Yet he takes issue with Willy's insistence upon being well liked. Salesmen, he says, sell products, not themselves, and successful men are not always the most lovable types. Charley is also sharp enough to see that Willy is toying with the idea of suicide. He tries to dissuade him but Willy hardly listens. All in all, Charley stands for sensible action rather than big talk.

PLOT DEVELOPMENT. In refusing Charley's job offer, Willy proudly cuts off a final chance to maintain some self-respect as a wage-earner. In addition, in spite of himself, Charley's suggestion that his theory of being well liked is fallacious reduces his self-assurance still further. Finally, Charley's mention of the insurance premium turns his thoughts to suicide, even though he still hopes that Biff may have succeeded.

TECHNIQUE. This is played in the same stage area as the preceding scene.

IMPORTANT THEMES: IMPORTANCE OF BEING WELL LIKED. Charley denies Willy's idea that being popular is the key to success.

CORRUPTION OF MODERN BUSINESS. Willy has harsh things to say about Howard. Charley, however, is a good, humane businessman and yet disputes Willy's claim that personal associations count for much. In apparent contradiction, however, he offers his broken friend a job.

SYMBOL: THE BOTTLE OF BOURBON. This gift from Charley to the departing Bernard suggests a pleasant, friendly relationship between the two men, both fairly prosperous. It points up their easy-going camaraderie as opposed to the tense, strained feelings between Willy and Biff, both of whom are in a difficult economic position.

ACT II, SCENE 7

SUMMARY. Awaiting Biff and Willy for dinner at the restaurant, Happy impresses the waiter, Stanley, with his sophisticated manner. Then he suavely picks up an attractive young diner, Miss Forsythe, bragging about himself and his brother. She leaves to find a friend for Biff, who has just arrived. Biff, much upset, says that after his long wait Oliver failed to recognize him. He was, after all, never a salesman, just a clerk. Impulsively, later, Biff stole Oliver's pen and ran away. He wants to tell Willy that he now realizes his limitations. But Happy warns him not to ruin Willy's hopes.

CHARACTER ANALYSES

HAPPY. This is Happy's scene. He shows a certain practiced deftness and savoir-faire in dealing with the waiter and the young prostitute, but he lies continually. There is also something cheap and second-rate in his pretensions to urbanity. He does, however, seem to be genuinely fond of his brother, and he is not without some consideration for Willy when he urges Biff not to tell him the worst. Of course, seeking the companionship of the two girls when he and Biff had asked Willy to dinner shows a certain thoughtlessness. But Happy has long concentrated upon sexual affairs, and, one feels, almost goes through the motions of setting up a date from force of habit.

BIFF. The taking of Oliver's pen recalls Biff's earlier stealing. But for all his disappointment, Biff here shows signs of growing up, of facing facts honestly. Yet in his eagerness to impart his new knowledge to Willy, thus clearing up any misapprehensions the older man may possess, he does not seem to consider at all the effect this might have upon an individual as distracted as Willy is now.

PLOT DEVELOPMENT. Biff's determination to tell Willy how insignificant the Oliver interview made him feel will prove highly disturbing to his already desperate father. In addition the date with the two girls, rather inconsiderately set up by Happy, will provide a tempting escape for the two sons when Willy's erratic actions prove embarrassing.

TECHNIQUE. The restaurant scene, also played on the front part of the stage, is suggested by light with a reddish glow, the music of a brassy orchestra, and a table and chairs brought on by the waiter and Happy.

IMPORTANT THEMES: QUESTIONABLE MORALITY. Happy boasts about his brother as a big cattleman and as a professional football star. He also tells of his mythical stay at West Point. He urges Biff to go on lying to their father. Biff, of course, has stolen again, but now he wants to admit the truth about himself.

CORRUPTION OF MODERN BUSINESS. The waiter is pleased to hear from Happy that the latter plans to go into business with his brother. In his place the bartender is always stealing from the boss.

FAMILY SOLIDARITY. Happy gets Biff a date, praising him highly. Happy tries to keep Willy happily anticipating Biff's success, while Biff thinks he will be better if he sees that Biff has failed from his own limitations and not merely to spite his father.

STEALING. Biff takes Oliver's fountain pen. This time, however, he does not pass off his action lightly. He is horrified and ashamed.

SYMBOLS: CHAMPAGNE. Happy makes much of his "overseas" champagne cocktail recipe, and sends the girl champagne to start up an acquaintance. This is obviously a proof of Happy's Continental elegance and one of his symbols of sophistication.

THE FOUNTAIN PEN. Oliver's personal pen is the sign of his executive status, something used to sign important documents. Biff, after a long wait, has been humiliatingly ignored. Taking the pen, a status symbol, is apparently almost an instinctive way of compensating for his injured pride. But the very irrationality of the act also helps to rouse Biff to realize the lie he has long been living.

ACT II, SCENE 8

SUMMARY. Willy joins them, and they order drinks. Already mildly intoxicated, Biff tries to tell Willy the grim facts, but both boys are shocked to hear that Willy has lost his job. From then on, Willy goes on assuming that Oliver welcomed Biff, and Happy encourages this delusion. Biff wavers between keeping Willy cheerful and admitting the dismal truth. Finally, Willy gets angry, and Biff gives up.

CHARACTER ANALYSES

WILLY. Bereft of all hopes and anxious to bring Linda back some good news, Willy wants only reassuring words from Biff, and therefore he angrily berates him whenever he tries to give an honest account. Willy always was enough of an optimist to make the most of the slightest encouraging sign. But here his own despair makes him try to find matter for rejoicing where none whatsoever exists. Because he is attempting the impossible, his temper is soon out of control, and he becomes increasingly harder to soothe.

BIFF. Anxious to reveal the new truths he has painfully discovered, Biff is also distressed to see his father so depressed and distraught. In addition, he is used over the years to having his mind made up for him by the strong-willed older man. Thus he finds it hard to speak his piece. Furthermore, feeling the effects of what he has been drinking, he is not altogether in a reasonable frame of mind. So as Willy continues to bait him, he finally gives up trying.

HAPPY. Happy's one concern is to calm Willy down. With this in mind, he lies continually, regardless of what Biff says, to let Willy go on thinking that Biff favorably impressed Oliver.

PLOT DEVELOPMENT. Willy's last hope has now been shattered. Excited and irritable, he will become hopelessly unmanageable and thus make impossible what was to have been a pleasant dinner party with his sons.

TECHNIQUE. This is a straight present-day scene played at the front of the stage as was the previous one.

IMPORTANT THEMES: IMPORTANCE OF BEING WELL LIKED. Willy is certain that Oliver must have remembered Biff, because Biff formerly impressed him.

FAMILY SOLIDARITY. Willy wants good news so that Linda will suffer less. The boys are sorry for him and want to calm him. Biff favors telling him the truth; Happy leans toward the reassuring lie.

QUESTIONABLE MORALITY. Willy does not want to hear that Biff was a mere shipping clerk, not a salesman. Happy lies repeatedly about the Oliver interview.

SYMBOL: THE BURNING WOODS. Willy uses this image more than once to distinguish between the threatening total catastrophe and mere minor setbacks.

ACT II, SCENE 9

SUMMARY. As Biff talks, Willy, distracted, hears young Bernard announcing to Linda that Biff failed mathematics and has gone to Boston to see Willy. The present-day Biff, bewildered by his father's talk of the old math failure, tries to tell him about the fountain pen. Willy slips back into his Boston memory. He is being paged in a hotel and his woman companion urges him to open the door. Biff meanwhile has been unable to make Willy see why he cannot return to talk again to Oliver. Finally, the girls return, and Willy staggers off to the men's room. Unable to cope with him further, Biff leaves, imploring Happy to stay. Happy, however, disowns his father and follows Biff with the two prostitutes after paying the bill.

CHARACTER ANALYSES

WILLY. In relatively lucid moments, Willy tries to coach Biff how to lie to Oliver about having gone off with his pen. He does everything possible to avoid facing facts, and when he can no longer do so, he bitterly denounces Biff. Actually, however, in this scene he is becoming increasingly distraught, since he keeps drifting back to the Boston episode in the past.

BIFF. Confused by Willy's references to events long ago, Biff still tries to explain why he cannot again approach Oliver. Yet as Willy eyes him accusingly, Biff seems the small boy again denying that he intended to steal at all. Afterwards, alarmed at Willy's condition, Biff resorts again to less disturbing lies. But he still wants to tell Willy the truth. Eventually, unable to stand the tensions and having been struck and called names by Willy, Biff goes off. Before leaving, however, he tells the girls that Willy is really a prince.

HAPPY. Before going, Biff asks Happy to look after Willy. When the younger son demurs, Biff accuses him of not caring for their father. Happy is angered, with some justice, for he has at least made some attempts to help Willy. Yet a moment later, he goes off with the girls and even denies that Willy is his father at all. In general, he is colder than Biff. Whereas the older brother flees in agony, Happy is off to salvage a good time. Essentially, however, both reveal a certain immaturity and cowardice in so deserting the disagreeable but sadly disturbed Willy.

PLOT DEVELOPMENT. As his despair increases through Biff's revelations, Willy becomes more and more upset. His mind recalls the unhappy past when Biff failed and the Boston episode wrecked their happy relationship. Obviously, being deserted now by his sons will do nothing to restore his emotional balance. Some critics, incidentally, have questioned the plausibility both of the datting of the girls by Happy and of the abandoning of Willy by the sons. Others see it as one more evidence of the same immaturity that has kept Biff moving from job to job and Happy forever telling lies.

TECHNIQUE. This is a complicated scene technically. A soft, misty light comes up on the house as young Bernard announces Biff's failure to Linda. A trumpet note indicates that Willy has a sudden, sharp recollection. "Hearing" young Bernard's announcement, Willy in the present abuses the older Biff. Again, as they argue further, the laughter of the Boston woman is heard from the left of the stage. Willy talks sometimes to the Boston telephone operator, sometimes to the woman, sometimes to the present-day Biff.

IMPORTANT THEMES: FATHER-SON CONFLICT. When Biff tries to tell Willy the truth, Willy accuses him of spiting him and of being nothing but a "rotten little louse." Biff tries to calm him and even to see him as he used to appear to him a "pal," or a "good companion." But the relationship is now merely a torment. So Biff leaves.

QUESTIONABLE MORALITY. Willy insists that Biff lie to Oliver about taking the pen. Happy tells the girls that Willy is not his father. Biff, of course, as well as Happy, walks aways from the disturbed Willy, who was their invited guest.

SYMBOL: THE RUBBER TUBE. Before leaving, Biff takes out the tubing and shows it to Happy. He asks Happy to stop Willy from killing himself, but Happy refuses the assignment while not denying that such is Willy's intent.

ACT II, SCENE 10

SUMMARY. In this flashback, Willy is sharing a hotel room with the Boston woman, Miss Francis. Repeated knocking at the door causes Willy to open it, after first sending her to wait in the bathroom. Biff has come to confess his failure and beg Willy to talk to his teacher, Mr. Birnbaum. He admits having missed the class and made fun of his teacher. The woman comes in, to Biff's horror, and Willy tries to invent a plausible explanation. The woman leaves but first demands her promised gift of stockings. Biff sobs, and Willy tries desperately to win him over, insisting that he was lonely. Biff, however, calls him a liar and a fake and says he does not want to go to the University. Back in the present, Stanley, the waiter, tells Willy that his sons have left. Willy tips him lavishly and sets out oddly to buy seeds.

CHARACTER ANALYSES

WILLY.   Even before Biff arrives, Willy is uneasy in the hotel. The knocking unnerves him, and the woman describes him as unhappy and selfish. Unexpectedly encountering Biff, he tries to bluff his way out of an embarrassing situation and all but throws the woman out. When all else fails, he resorts to the truth. But by then Biff is sadly disillusioned. As for Biff's failure, it is significant that Willy at this point does not blame Biff. In fact, he enjoys his account of how he mockingly imitated the teacher's lisp and is annoyed that Bernard did not furnish enough answers. His love for Biff is apparent throughout, but his behavior gives the boy some cause to consider him a liar.

BIFF.   Young Biff first shows here a childish faith that his father can talk the teacher into giving him the points he needs to graduate. The minute he has trouble, he runs off to get help from Dad. His thinking, too, is immature: the course was failed because the teacher hated him. When afterwards Biff discovers his father's liaison, he bursts into angry tears, will listen to no explanation, and calls his fallen idol names. He is particularly distressed that Willy has given the buyer "Mama's stockings." And now that his faith has been shattered, he will do nothing about summer school and does not want to go to the University at all. There is heartbreak and disillusionment here. But Biff seems to react like a small child, rather than a young man of college age. Willy has, of course, always played the hero in front of Biff. Now Biff passionately denounces him as a fraud.

PLOT DEVELOPMENT.   From Biff's first references in Act I to Willy as a "fake," an explanation has been forthcoming. Bernard's references to Boston and his question about what happened there increased the suspense. This scene explains the tensions between Willy and Biff and suggests why Biff never went on to succeed when he seemed to have such bright prospects. As a memory it involves deep feelings of guilt on Willy's part, and his reliving it at this time probably increases his sense of being lost. Some commentators have doubted that the revelation of Willy's extramarital affair could really have had such a cataclysmic effect on a normally resilient young man. Others justify this as plausible on the grounds that Willy's dubious "training" had given Biff no adequate preparation for coping with the realities of a far from perfect world. In other words, discovering Willy's perfidy was probably the bitterest possible blow that Biff could have received. But he would sooner or later have reacted similarly to other inevitable rude awakenings.

TECHNIQUE. The sensual aspect of Willy's affair is suggested by the type of musical background played. The scene is played at the front of the stage, and lighting is used to pick out the principal figures. There is otherwise no hotel-room set or furnishings.

IMPORTANT THEMES: FATHER-SON CONFLICT. Willy has done nothing directly to injure Biff. He wants only to help his son get to college. But Biff has had his illusions wrecked and is both miserable and furious. The moment before, he was blithely confident that Dad could fix anything, even a failing mark. From now on, however, the idyll is over. Biff and Willy will quarrel heatedly, be partially reconciled, then quarrel again.

THE IMPORTANCE OF BEING WELL LIKED. Biff assures Willy that if he talks to Birmbaum in his impressive fashion, the teacher will alter the grade. Willy, for his part, enjoys hearing how Biff mimicked the teacher to the great delight of his admiring classmates.

QUESTIONABLE MORALITY. Biff has no compunction about having missed classes or cheated on exams. He is only sorry that he let his father down. Willy is annoyed that Bernard did not cheat more efficiently so that Biff could have passed. Willy lies to Biff about the woman in his room, and finally excuses his actions on the grounds that he was lonely.

SYMBOLS: THE STOCKINGS. Throughout the play Willy has been uneasy whenever he sees Linda, who has little money, darning old stockings. The boxes he gives Miss Francis are partially a business investment, for she can get him in to see buyers. They also make Willy a generous, desirable man to know and thus make him feel like the "big shot" he wants to be. To Biff, however, they represent an insult to his mother. And they thus aggravate his bitterness regarding Willy's deception.

SEEDS. Willy asks the waiter where he can buy seeds. He wants something to grow in his garden. He has just been deserted by his sons, and in a sense they were his plants, his future growth.

Now he will try once more to raise vegetables from the ground, so that something that is his will grow and flourish.

ACT II, SCENE 11

SUMMARY.   Arriving home late with roses as a peace offering, the boys are met by a bitterly indignant Linda. Throwing down the flowers, she denounces the pair for deserting their father and tells both to pack and leave. Happy tries lying to gloss over the situation. Biff is remorseful and contrite. He begs to see his father before he goes. Willy, however, is out planting vegetables.

CHARACTER ANALYSES

LINDA.   Unyielding, almost ferocious in her denunciation of her sons, Linda will listen to no excuses. Willy is her one concern. She is more wife than mother, although she sometimes seems to mother Willy. Seemingly meek and uncomplaining whenever her husband speaks, she is here hard, relentless, even somewhat coarse. Only when she suddenly fears that she cannot by strong words stop Biff from harassing Willy further, does she adopt a milder tone and actually beg. Some critics have wondered whether or not such a positive, uncompromising woman would be likely to take so much verbal abuse from the moody Willy. Is it just that she loves him more than she does her sons? It may be noted, of course, that even though she talks soothingly to Willy, she keeps close accounts of the finances and does tend to run his life. It was she who did battle with Ben, and it was she who promoted the meeting with Howard.

HAPPY.   A little afraid of the irate Linda, Happy tries as usual to lie his way out of difficulties. His assurance that Willy actually had a good time with them is obviously implausible, for Willy has come home before them. But Happy is forever trying to keep others satisfied by making free with the facts. When his lies fail to convince, he goes upstairs without apology.

BIFF.   As opposed to his essentially more thick-skinned brother, Biff is conscience-stricken. He does try to tell Linda that Willy is not yet dying, but he makes no serious effort to defend his own actions. He also rudely cuts off Happy's attempts to suggest that Willy did have a pleasant evening. Humbled and remorseful, Biff still insists upon seeing Willy. And Linda is forced to recognize that Biff, too, can on occasion be a determined individual.

PLOT DEVELOPMENT.   Linda's ultimatum that the boys must leave will hasten the crucial scene between Biff and Willy that will lead to the latter's suicide. The scene also reveals vital differences in the personalities of the two sons. Morally, there is some hope for Biff, little for Happy.

TECHNIQUE. This scene is played in the kitchen and living room of the house. Lighting is used effectively, especially when the boys, fearful, discover that Linda knows what has happened and she moves toward them furiously.

IMPORTANT THEMES: FAMILY SOLIDARITY. Linda has no qualms about insisting that the boys take responsibility for Willy. In view of the fact that Willy is not well and was their guest, she is obviously justified here. But, throughout, this emphasis upon obligations of parent to grown son and grown son to parent is quite pronounced. Charley and Bernard talk of letting things go and walking away. This the Lomans, with the exception of Happy, cannot seem to accept.

QUESTIONABLE MORALITY. Linda denounces the desertion of Willy as cruel and inhuman. Happy goes on lying to make Linda less angry and to make things easier for him and Biff. Linda also has harsh words for their dealing with the two prostitutes, although Happy assures her, probably truthfully for once, that all he and the girls did was follow the morose Biff and try to cheer him up.

SYMBOLS: THE ROSES. Ordinarily an attractive, fairly expensive present, these would probably be welcomed by Linda, who, as Willy has indicated, has had her share of trouble. But she roughly pushes them out of Happy's hands. As she declared in the beginning, she will not remain on friendly terms with anyone who is unkind to Willy. In rejecting the roses, she is rejecting her sons because of their having hurt her husband.

THE GARDEN. Like the seeds, in the previous scene, this is Willy's pathetic attempt to start something for the future. When Ben offered him the Alaska post, he told him he was building his fortune through his sales work. He also looked to Biff to carry on the Loman name with distinction. Now both of these hopes have faded. So in the dead of night he is out planting vegetables.

ACT II, SCENE 12

SUMMARY. Busy planting carrots and lettuce by flashlight, Willy starts consulting a vision of Ben about killing himself for his twenty-thousand-dollar insurance money. Ben admits that this is a substantial sum but wonders about the certainty of payment and about Willy's being called a coward. Willy, however, sees

the act as giving Biff a "diamond." Biff would also be impressed by Willy's funeral, with mourners from distant states. But Ben
frightens him by suggesting that Biff might only hate him.

CHARACTER ANALYSES

WILLY.   Here Willy, gardening in the dark, is hardly rational.
He is, however, obsessed with the idea of leaving a great sum
to Biff. Presumably if Biff sees that his father is able to give
him such a sum, then Biff will stop spiting Willy and make a
success of his life. Then, after all, Willy will be assured of a sort
of immortality. Willy thinks of Ben in connection with this insurance project because it involves a large fortune made instan-
taneously—a found "diamond," not small sums made through
endless appointments. Ben also would not be one to show over-
concern about the morality of the proposition. Yet, even considering the act in "practical" terms, Willy is not sure how Biff
will judge him. And he does not merely want Biff to have the
money. He also wants Biff to honor his memory. So in considering the possibility of committing suicide, Willy wants to be able
to leave something to Biff, and also to Linda who "has suffered."
But he is also, as the Boston woman long ago suggested, "self-
centered" enough to want proper recognition for the sacrifice of
his life. As for the morality of suicide, or of cheating insurance
companies, Willy is not concerned.

For Willy has a child's view of what is fair and unfair. He has
had to work hard over the years to pay his premiums. The least
the company can do is pay him if he's willing to kill himself for
money.

BEN.   In earlier scenes Willy's memories may or may not represent the older brother, Ben, as he actually was in life. Here Ben
is clearly a figment, an imaginary being. In the debate over suicide,
he is actually that side of Willy's personality that has always admired swift, decisive action and looked for wealth to be obtained
in an audacious coup. In addition, "Ben" always seems to personify
a certain lawlessness, an impatience with the stricter requirements
of ethics. And Willy has never been overly scrupulous about the
property of others. Yet "Ben" also stands for a combination of
selfishness and hard-headed practicality. This type of mind can
appreciate material wealth in the form of diamonds or cash in lump
sums. But it is skeptical about building a business through friendly
contacts or counting upon a son's admiration for a suicide father.
As both materialist and man of action, the "Ben" side finds self-
destruction a rather negative course, and is cynical enough to
wonder whether or not it would pay off at all. Speaking in his own
person, Willy has some generous concern for Linda and Biff, as

well as an egotistic urge to prove that he is known to many. Yet the adventurous, opportunistic "Ben" in him that prompts him to a final desperate undertaking also with its cold skepticism stays his hand.

PLOT DEVELOPMENT. Suicide has been hinted previously. Linda has spoken of other attempts to the boys; Biff has found the rubber tubing; and Charley has keenly noted Willy's reference to his being worth more dead than alive. Here, however, the plan is seen actually taking form. Willy's death thus seems imminent. Yet for the moment worries about Biff's possible reaction postpone the move. The very fact, of course, that Willy is conversing with a long-dead brother and not merely remembering indicates considerable mental disturbance.

TECHNIQUE. This scene takes place in the garden, that is, on the apron or front part of the stage. A soft blue light suggests the darkness of night and little of the surroundings can be seen. Willy uses a flashlight to read the directions on his seed packets and occasionally uses a hoe. Ben appears out of the darkness to the right. The scene is also interesting in that this is the first time that Willy holds a discussion with a figure from his past. Hitherto he has apparently just relived crucial experiences, although sometimes commenting upon them in a manner that confuses present-day characters, as when he talks to the grown Biff about failing in school.

IMPORTANT THEMES: FAMILY SOLIDARITY. Willy can talk only to his brother Ben. He wants to kill himself so that Linda and Biff will have what he can give them.

THE IMPORTANCE OF BEING WELL LIKED. Biff will be impressed to see how well known Willy was, when all the old friends who liked him came from New England and elsewhere to attend his funeral. Willy is again engaging in grandiose visions. In fact, no one will come except family and the two neighbors.

QUESTIONABLE MORALITY. Willy seems unconcerned about any moral aspects to the question of taking one's own life. To him it is not cowardly. Yet he would not want to have Biff think him a coward or a fool. He also has no worries about whether or not he may be guilty of fraud as far as the insurance claim is concerned.

LAMENT FOR THE PAST. Willy recalls poignantly the days when the healthy young Biff used to enjoy winter sports and carry his sample cases and polish the car. How, he asks, can one recover such peaks of happiness?

SYMBOLS: SEEDS.   As before, Willy's absurd planting operation represents his desperate urge to accomplish something, to build a future for his heirs.

DIAMONDS.   These have throughout been Willy's symbol for great, satisfying wealth—beautiful and impressive. Here he equates his diamond with money to be paid his family by the insurance company if he kills himself. It would prove him a man worth respecting, and it would be a dazzlingly large lump sum, not little amounts pieced together by endless selling appointments.

ACT II, SCENE 13

SUMMARY.   Biff joins Willy in the garden and tells him he is leaving for good. Uneasy about facing Linda and furious that Biff will not try again to see Oliver, Willy refuses a goodbye handshake. He curses Biff for spiting him. Stung, Biff takes out the rubber tube and calls Willy a fake. As Linda and Happy watch helpless, Biff says he was in jail for stealing in Kansas City. He has always stolen because Willy made him think he must be important in a hurry. He is through running. He will go back to the West, to the work he likes. Both he and his father must face it that they are not leaders. Willy denies this irately, but Biff, no longer angry, sobs brokenly. All he asks is that Willy burn his false dreams.

CHARACTER ANALYSES

WILLY.   Willy here is seen roused to fury and bitterness by his sense of guilt. If Biff is failing, Biff must be still taking revenge for the Boston disillusionment because if Biff is *not* failing deliberately, then Willy is to blame, and that sort of burden Willy cannot shoulder. If, however, Biff has become a drifter out of spite, then Willy, however outraged by such ingratitude and meanness, can see himself as blameless by comparison. One lapse on his part obviously did not deserve such a long campaign of calculated insult and retribution. The third explanation, offered by Biff, namely, that he never possessed the extraordinary potential attributed to him by Willy and hence would under no circumstances have been a great leader, is almost equally obnoxious to Willy. For if Biff does not succeed magnificently, then Biff is nothing. But if Biff is nothing, so is Willy. And Willy has spent a lifetime covering up the discouraging smallness of his income by picturing himself as a dynamic, aggressive salesman universally admired and Biff as the heir apparent who would easily surpass even his father's enviable record. If he accepts Biff's less flattering appraisal of both, then he must not only give up the emotional props on which he has relied over the years. He must also admit that even if his Boston affair did not wreck Biff, his "training" of his son, of which he was so proud, left his son inadequately prepared for life. This idea, again demanding an admission of guilt, is equally insupportable. So Willy, with no job and no future, and fearful of losing all remaining shreds of self-esteem, shouts imprecations at the relentless Biff. Biff may hope to stave off Willy's suicide by making his father come to terms with reality. Willy, however, recoils with horror and fury when Biff attacks his foolish illusions.

BIFF. Highly emotional throughout this whole climactic scene, Biff's first objective is to take leave of Willy amicably, thus putting an end to the quarrels that are causing both such agony. As Willy, however, not only refuses a parting blessing but angrily denounces Biff as spiteful, the younger man becomes irate in turn and insists upon destroying once and for all Willy's false picture of both of them. The more Willy tries to shy away from unpleasant truths, the more the now remorseless Biff tries to force them upon him. Biff starts by denying that he has any wish to blame Willy. But once roused by Willy's accusations of spite, he indicates that he sees that his repeated thefts, culminating in a jail term, are traceable to Willy's having created in him a false impression that he was never meant to be a subordinate, but always an executive. While he is at it, Biff also points out that Happy is not an assistant buyer as he claims but only one of those helping the assistant buyer. In this scene Biff does show some progress toward maturity. He no longer has quite so unrealistic a picture of his own capabilities as he had. He says that he is through with stealing, and he also has recognized the kind of outdoor life he wants and will pursue it presumably without making impossible demands of it. At the same time, he still reveals some traits that do not suggest an adult personality. For one thing, he is not in command of his emotions. At one moment he is ready to strike Willy, and shortly thereafter he breaks down and sobs. Secondly, he is all too ready, when under fire, to shunt the blame onto Willy for his own criminal acts. It was Willy's fault that he stole. Finally, he tends to go to extremes. He and Willy may not be the extraordinary people Willy always envisioned, but whether they are a "dime a dozen," or even "nothing," is debatable.

PLOT DEVELOPMENT. Willy has regarded his projected suicide as a grand gesture that will marvelously impress Biff. Here Biff, in taking out the rubber tube and flinging it at Willy, denies that he will regard Willy as any hero at all. Taken with the doubts expressed by "Ben," this would seem to be a deterrent. In this scene also, however, Biff tries to make Willy give up his self-important delusions. There is no indication that he succeeds. Willy may still go ahead with his plan. Linda and Happy seem increasingly unable to influence either Biff or Willy.

TECHNIQUE. Played partially out on the stage apron (the garden), the scene moves into the kitchen. There are no flashbacks. In terms of dramatic structure, this is a great "confrontation scene," in which two antagonists face each other and take up some vital issue to settle once and for all. It might also be termed a "necessary scene." There has been much in the play about the relationship of Willy and Biff, and Biff has been relatively reticent although he has indicated the hostility he feels. Here we learn some of his true feelings, that the play, in a sense, has been promising all along.

IMPORTANT THEMES: FATHER-SON CONFLICT. Willy tries to blame Biff for spitefully refusing to succeed. Biff claims that Willy's false teaching encouraged him to steal and also to be confused about his true nature. He also calls his father a fake for toying with the idea of suicide.

QUESTIONABLE MORALITY. Biff reveals that he served a three-month jail term for stealing a suit. He blames Willy for having given him false teaching. He accuses Happy of lying and says that in the Loman house, no one ever told the truth.

SYMBOLS: THE RUBBER TUBE. To Biff this proves Willy a fraud and no hero. If Willy kills himself, Biff will have no pity for him.

THE FOUNTAIN PEN. Representing to Biff the life of a business executive, Oliver's pen now seems to him the symbol of all that he wants to reject—the stealing and the running away, the whole business world. He is going back instead to the Western open-air work that he finds satisfying.

ACT II, SCENE 14

SUMMARY. Convinced by Biff's agonized sobs that his son loves him, Willy again sees Ben and thinks of the twenty thousand dollars. Happy, promising his mother that he'll get married, goes upstairs. Linda, after pleading with Willy to join her, follows. After she goes, Willy talks to Ben about Biff's magnificence with all that money. Ben agrees that Willy would be fetching a diamond out of the jungle. Willy thinks once more of Biff's football glory and then after a momentary panic rushes off. After the musical suggestion of a crash, the family are preparing for Willy's funeral.

CHARACTER ANALYSES

WILLY. Despite the harsh words uttered in fear and anger, Willy shows here his deep love for Biff. He also still has his vision of Biff as magnificent and will realize it by getting his son the insurance money. Willy also takes tender leave of Linda, sorry that she is so tired. He is hopeful now that everything will work out for the best. In carrying off the "proposition," he will have succeeded himself and made success possible for Biff, thus pulling victory out of defeat. He is fearful but triumphant. He is also not quite sane.

LINDA.   Having made her peace with her sons, Linda fearfully suspects what Willy intends to do. Yet she goes off and leaves the distracted man alone. The only preparation for this action has been her custom of leaving the rubber tubing where it was when Willy was home to help preserve his dignity. Linda does not want Willy to kill himself, but apparently cannot bring herself to interfere in order to stop him. There may be some question of plausibility here, but if Willy were determined enough, presumably he could kill himself sometime. And the requirements of drama are probably better satisfied by having the action occur at this time.

PLOT DEVELOPMENT.   By an ironic twist Biff's impassioned plea, intended to convince Willy that he is a "nothing," hence not worth the sacrifice of someone's life, has just the opposite effect. Suddenly certain of Biff's love, Willy sees his son as "magnificent," needing only wealth to far outdistance Bernard. Thus he is now convinced that suicide is the answer and receives confirmation from the vision of "Ben" that this is the way to get diamonds out of the jungle.

TECHNIQUE.   Light and sound effects are used here to suggest first of all Willy's distraction and momentary panic. Then music conveys the idea of a car crash and subsequently makes the transition necessary to start the family toward Willy's funeral. The grave is supposedly located at the center front of the stage apron. Thus when the characters talk around the grave, they seem almost to be talking directly to the audience.

IMPORTANT THEMES: FAMILY SOLIDARITY.   Willy by his suicide will give Biff the chance for magnificence. Linda speaks encouragingly about both sons and indicates her love for Willy. As the funeral music starts, the family moves together, joined by Bernard and Charley.

IMPORTANCE OF PHYSICAL PROWESS.   Willy's last vision of Biff is as the football hero. Biff's football is important and important people are watching him. Biff's skill at the game is still a vital element in his father's concept of his magnificence.

SYMBOLS: THE JUNGLE. Ben keeps talking of taking diamonds out of the jungle. The jungle to Willy seems to be the world in general that has made it hard for him to get ahead. The money he gets through his suicide will make jungle fighting easier for Biff. At the same time Willy has seen himself, as he remarked to Howard, as coming of a race of adventurous men with a streak of self-reliance. Such men—Ben included—tame jungles and are not tamed by them. And here Willy conquers his.

DIAMONDS. Again the insurance money is equated with diamonds. There is, first of all, a splendor about such stones, and Willy means his death to be a noble gesture. Secondly, they suggest great wealth, not small sums—and twenty thousand is more than Willy has ever had. Finally, they are made to represent a prize won by daring and initiative, by the bold stroke of an adventurous spirit. And this, too, is the way Willy regards the money he wants to leave Biff. Incidentally, the play never reveals whether or not Biff ever gets the money. It is never again mentioned.

REQUIEM

SUMMARY. Only Linda, her sons and Charley and Bernard join at Willy's grave. Linda laments that no one else came to the funeral. She cannot understand Willy's suicide when they were almost free of debt and their needs were small. Biff remembers sadly the good old days when they all repaired the house, but insists that Willy's dreams were wrong. Charley defends Willy as a true salesman "riding on a smile and a shoeshine." Biff, unconvinced, invites Happy to head West with him. But Happy is determined to realize Willy's dream in the city. Linda, kneeling, sorrowfully bids Willy farewell. Weeping, she goes off with Biff.

CHARACTER ANALYSES

LINDA. Linda expresses here the tender grief of one who had a deep love for Willy. Even if not a well-known or well-liked man—since not a single business acquaintance comes to his funeral—Willy was still someone who was loved and missed. Yet unless a certain difficulty in comprehending may be allowed in the person suddenly bereaved, Linda's comments are curious. Her remarks, for instance, to the effect that Willy's act is inexplicable because they were "free and clear" do not sound like those of the woman who was always ready to cite facts and figures and presumably knew that Willy had lost his job. From the first she knew about Willy's suicidal notions and earlier had offered some possible explanations to the boys. In terms of the drama, however, her expression of sorrow and loss is usually quite affecting.

BIFF.   This scene shows that Biff has not changed his position. He can remember warmly and pleasurably the early days when Willy and his boys fixed the stoop and added a new porch. But sorrow over Willy's death has not altered his conviction that Willy's basic point of view was wrong. He is still, as he declared before, going back out West where he has been happiest. And he even tries to coax Happy into going with him. As Charley's defense of Willy suggests, Biff is still perhaps too intolerant. Must Willy's dreams have been "all, all wrong"? But Biff at least has solved his own dilemma and can now go back to his ranch life, without feeling guilty because he is not making a name for himself in the urban business world that he so hates.

HAPPY.   Not unaffected by his father's death, Happy still voices the old Loman dream "to come out number one." Yet his references to not being "licked," and to showing everybody in the "racket" suggest that eventually he, too, may be headed for disaster. For Happy throughout the play has shown no inclination to work harder than ever or do his job more efficiently. All his talk has been of getting away with bribes and seducing other men's fiancées, of being slickly "covered" for unauthorized time off and of feeling nothing but contempt for those giving him orders. Even in the crucial scene of the showdown, he objected when Biff pointed out that he was only one of two assistants to the assistant buyer. Despite occasional pledges to get married, Happy does not seem to have changed at all. So his blithe assurances that he will "beat this racket" seem discouragingly hollow.

CHARLEY.   In defending the man who always tended to insult him, Charley shows considerable understanding of the demands of a salesman's line of work. His line about "a smile and a shoe-shine" is one of the most famous in the entire play. And Charley throughout has been a sympathetic, helpful neighbor. Yet, in a way, Charley's eulogy is confusing. For before this he tried to change Willy. He insisted, for instance, that being "well-liked" was not that important, and more than once he told Willy to "grow up." The play itself seems to point up the foolish side of Willy's visions rather than the creative side that might make a man succeed in Willy's line of work. Like Linda's tearful laments, Charley's words do add a nice touch of sentiment. And they are appropriate, probably, to the kindly old friend. But essentially they only make one lament Willy's passing and brush aside whatever critical approach has hitherto been taken.

PLOT DEVELOPMENT.   The plot virtually ends with Willy's suicide. Apart from the sad or elegiac tapering off here, however, this scene rounds out the story of Willy's sons. Happy will go on following Willy's none too practical course. Biff, rejecting Willy's dream, will pursue his own less demanding objectives.

TECHNIQUE.   As previously indicated, holding the requiem scene at the very front of the stage seems to bring the audience into closer contact with those making final comments. The flute music at the end and the lighting that throws into relief the tall, almost menacing apartment buildings also add their own subtle interpretive effects.

IMPORTANT THEMES: IMPORTANCE OF PHYSICAL PROWESS.   Biff remembers happily the work with their hands that gave the Loman men such satisfaction. Charley and Linda agree nostalgically that Willy was excellent when manual skills were demanded.

FATHER-SON CONFLICT.   Even though Willy is dead, Biff is still arguing with him. He condemns Willy's dreams at Willy's grave and tries to get his brother to give up the impossible struggle for impressive wealth and fame.

CORRUPTION OF MODERN BUSINESS.   The terms in which Happy alludes to the city world—the "racket," in which he is going to show everybody that he can come out on top—recall all that has previously been said about the intense competition and low moral standards. By contrast, Biff's call to join him in the more easy-going West sounds like a last chance for health and sanity.

LAMENT FOR THE PAST.   Biff remembers affectionately the old days when Willy and the boys worked happily together to fix up the house.

SYMBOL: THE HOUSE.   Linda, always the woman of the house, is particularly saddened to think that now that the mortgage has been finally paid off, Willy will not be there to share the building with her. In a sense, the house represents the whole of their thirty-five hard-working years together. Their marriage has been the struggle to possess a house. Biff, too, refers to parts of the house, such as stoop, cellar, and porch. To him they represent Willy's expert carpentering skills, and hence the answer to his unrealistic or wrong dreams. And they also signify the good years of cooperative effort when family harmony prevailed.

ANALYSES OF MAJOR CHARACTERS

WILLY LOMAN: In a sense there are two Willy Lomans in this play. There is the present broken, exhausted man in his sixties, soon to end his life. And there is the more confident, vigorous Willy of some fifteen years before, who appears in the flashbacks. One actor portrays both, readily shifting from one representation to the other. To some extent, of course, the personality remains constant. The younger Willy, although given to boastful blustering, does admit misgivings to Linda and loneliness to Biff. And the shattered older man, in turn, occasionally reverts to his former manner of jaunty optimism. Yet the changes are great and significant. The earlier Willy could never have been the idol of his teen-aged sons had he behaved in the perverse, distracted fashion of his older self.

Willy's agitation during his last days stems from a twofold sense of failure. He has not been able to launch successfully in the world his beloved son Biff, and he no longer can meet the demands of his own selling job. Although not altogether ignoring Linda and Happy, he is primarily concerned about the once magnificent young football star who at thirty-four drifts from one temporary ranch job to the next. Willy cannot "walk away" from Biff's problem, as Bernard suggests, nor can he accept Linda's view that "life is a casting off." Being over sixty, Willy is doubtless tiring physically. The sample cases are heavy. The seven-hundred-mile drives are arduous. And many business contacts, developed over the years, are vanishing as the men of his era die or retire. Yet the worry over Biff has obviously accelerated his collapse.

Actually, Willy's attitude toward Biff is complex. On the one hand, there is a strong personal attachment. He wants Biff to love him. He remembers yearningly the fondness shown for him by Biff as a boy, and he still craves this. At this point, however, relations are strained. Although Willy shies away from remembering so painful an episode, he knows in his heart that the Boston affair left the boy bitterly disillusioned. Feeling some sense of guilt, Willy fears that all of Biff's later difficulties may have been really attempts to get revenge. Biff has failed, in other words, mainly to "spite" Willy. Although outwardly resenting such alleged vindictiveness, Willy still wants to get back the old comradeship, even if he has to buy it dearly. "Why can't I give him something," he asks the spectral Ben, "and not have him hate me?" And his great final moment of joy and triumph occurs when he can exclaim, "Isn't that remarkable? Biff—he likes me!"

On the other hand, Willy also is emotionally involved with Biff because his son's success or failure is also his. By becoming rich and influential, the handsome, personable Biff was slated to provide Willy's victorious reply to all not sufficiently impressed with his own modest advancement. By making his fortune in the business world, Biff would prove that Willy had been right in turning down Ben's adventurous challenge to head for Alaska. He would also outshine the sensible, plodding Charley and Bernard, thus establishing once and for all Willy's theory that having personality and being "well liked" were the great requisites for preeminence. Losing his own job, Willy is naturally unhappy. But if he can still purchase success for Biff with the insurance money, he personally will yet have won. "I always knew one way or another we were gonna make it, Biff and I!"

If, however, Willy at any stage is apt to overindulge in grandiose daydreams, he is hardly the "phoney little fake" he once seems to the shocked Biff. He works steadily at one job for thirty-six years and does pay off a long-term mortgage, even if at the end he accepts some help from Charley. He takes good care of the house, too, capably making even major repairs. Although not altogether faithful, he is a reasonably satisfactory husband to Linda, who obviously respects him. He does not like to see her darn stockings or work too hard. And when he loses his job, he is sorry to think how much she has suffered. In his own way, too, he has the makings of an admirable father. He gives much attention to his boys, showing them how to do things, working with them, and praising their accomplishments. He roots for them at their games, and defends them loyally. When Biff fails, he pays for several correspondence courses, even though he has to pawn his prized diamond watch fob given him by Ben. And finally, there is genuine dignity in the man when he spiritedly speaks up for his rights with Howard.

Willy is partially a victim of circumstance. He could not have avoided getting old and tired, any more than he could have prevented the building of the apartments that hem in his house. There was even an element of mischance in Biff's inopportune visit to Boston. What's more, Willy did not originate some of the erroneous concepts and values that helped defeat him. The idea of the fast-made fortune, the "quick killing," is, to some extent, characteristically American. And our history certainly indicates that some did reach the top by combining personal attractiveness with

a casual disregard for ethical practice. Moreover, Willy was hardly the first in our society to overemphasize athletic prowess at the
expense of steady brain work.

Yet in placing excessive reliance upon these dubious success for-
mulas, Willy fails to take a realistic view of his limitations and
those of his son. By all but encouraging Biff's petty thievery and
giving it the flattering name of "initiative," he steers Biff toward
an eventual jail term and Happy toward the discreditable habit
of taking bribes. By running down the importance of good grades,
he prepares the way for Biff's disastrous failure. By harping upon
Uncle Ben's rapid rise to fortune, he builds in both boys a dis-
taste for the type of regular, fairly routine work that will not make
anyone, as Biff says, a "big shot boss in two weeks." Finally, by
encouraging them to idolize him through his blown-up accounts of
their situation, he does little to help them really mature. Toward
the end, Biff seems to be groping sadly toward some measure of
self-knowledge. But Happy is still determined to "beat this racket"
and come out "number one man." On the day of the big game,
Charley ruefully asks Willy when he is going to grow up. In some
ways Willy never does. His boyish enthusiasm is, of course, part
of his appeal. But his persistent refusal to face facts squarely
drives him at last to a violent death. Ironically, his suicide, to
him the ultimate in magnificent gestures, merely leaves Linda woe-
fully bereft and Biff more than ever sure that "he had the wrong
dreams. All, all wrong."

BIFF LOMAN: At thirty-four, this husky, good-looking former
star athlete is a moody, troubled man. Like Willy, he is worried
both about family tensions and about his work. He is fond of
his mother and saddened to see her looking older. And even
though he has never regained his idolizing reverence for Willy,
he would really like to meet him again on pleasant, amicable terms.
In all probability he also misses the high praise with which Willy
bolstered his self-confidence. Now, however, whenever he returns,
obviously no success, he dreads his father's disapproval and is
clearly on the defensive. Thus, when Willy "mocks" him and accuses him of failing out of spite, he is ready with an angry
rejoinder. This, in turn, makes Linda antagonistic, and Biff, feeling guilty and inept, is more depressed than ever.

Having relied apparently too much in boyhood years upon the
heady encouragement of an adored and adoring father, Biff seems
never to have recovered fully from the Boston disillusionment.
Bernard's account of Biff's burning of his "University of Virginia"
sneakers suggests the dramatic finality of Biff's renunciation of all
bright college plans. After that he takes various short courses but
always loses heart. The ranch work, on the other hand, does give

him some satisfaction. Away from his father's disappointed frowning, he likes the chance to use his physical strength in the open air.

Yet he makes very little money at such seasonal jobs, and keeps moving from one to another hoping for more. All the while, too, he cannot shake off his father's prediction of an extraordinarily great future for him. Trying better paying city work, he feels stifled by the routine and becomes impatient at the slowness of the rise to some position of security and respect. So he steals and runs off, engages in devising fantasy schemes for making a quick fortune, then drifts back to another dollar-an-hour cattle-herding stopgap. Even though this erratic program has left him increasingly anxious and disheartened, there is at least a faint hope for Biff. For Biff, at least, knows that he is "mixed-up" and wants to stop acting "like a boy." After the disastrous attempt to see Oliver, he does face bravely a few more harsh facts about his limitations and resolves to give up following the old "phony dream."

Actually, Biff, like Willy, always tends to go somewhat to extremes. So his passionate insistence, toward the end, that he is "nothing," or that he and his father are both "a dime a dozen," still sounds a little like the uncompromising disclaimer of the youngster who had sobbingly burned his sneakers. Now he sees his father's dreams as "All, all wrong." Yet if he still talks a little like the grandstand hero, he is still groping toward a more realistic, more mature self-appraisal. Neither Willy nor Happy ever gets even that far.

LINDA LOMAN: Like Kate Keller in *All My Sons*, Linda is primarily wife rather than mother. Or if she is motherly, her ministrations are for Willy rather than her sons. Except when it becomes necessary for her to remind him of unpaid bills, she is forever soothing him, flattering him, tactfully suggesting courses of action, and trying to get him to eat enough and get some rest. She is almost always patient and kind to him, ignoring his minor outbursts and considerately accepting without demur such obvious deceptions as the borrowing from Charley. Linda loves her husband, respects him as a steady, hard-working man, and regards his sufferings with compassion. But she humors him as a child rather than meeting him squarely as an adult.

Yet the same mild-mannered, gentle Linda can be surprisingly blunt and harsh when she talks to her sons. She may not ever challenge Willy's grandiose talk to his face, but she reveals a clear, tough-minded recognition of the true financial picture. She rebukes Biff for failing to keep in touch and orders him either to behave pleasantly to his father or to leave. And she can coolly describe

Happy as a "philandering bum." After the restaurant disaster, she denounces both fiercely, flings away their flowers and imperiously orders them out of the house. Except when they disturb or irritate Willy, she talks to them amiably enough. But she is simply not concerned about them. Her one thought is Willy. If their presence cheers him or helps him in some way, she is glad to have them around. But if what they do further upsets her already disturbed grown-up "child," then the sons must go and not return.

HAPPY LOMAN: This dashing "assistant to the assistant" buyer shares with Biff a fondness for rugged outdoor living but wants material success even more. He appears at first to have come to terms with life better than either his father or his brother. He has his own car and his own apartment. He has had considerable proof of his virile appeal to women, and has developed a glib line with which to impress them. In a small way, he is quite an accomplished liar and has all but convinced himself that he is slated to become the store's next merchandise manager.

Actually, he is by no means as well adjusted as he seems. For one thing, he cannot quiet down his own scruples. He knows that he is wrong when he takes bribes, and he has some sense of guilt as regards the seduction of other men's fiancées. In addition, he does appreciate the fact that the merchandise manager, whose success he so patently envies, is still discontented and restless. So he suspects that even reaching that pinnacle may not guarantee happiness. Moreover, he too, like Biff, feels indoor work confining. Also physically strong, he misses the exaltation of the athletic contest, and has a certain contempt for the weaklings with whom he must work.

Happy still has vestiges of old ideals. He objects to all that is false around him, even while being false himself. Even while picking up a prostitute, he remarks what a shame it is that there are so few good women. And he dreams of settling down with a decent girl like his mother. Although embarrassed by his father's odd behavior, he is not ungenerous. He did send Willy previously to Florida for a rest. And, of course, he is genuinely fond of Biff.

Yet he often refuses to face unpleasant truths and resists Biff's attempts to clear up misconceptions as bitterly as Willy does. Whatever occasional admissions he makes, he will not give up either his dream world or his shabby sensual affairs. He may talk of changing his ways and getting married, but he never sounds convincing. And his final act is to reject Biff's invitation to start anew, preferring to justify Willy's dream of coming out "number-one man." Unlike Biff, Happy learns relatively little from witnessing his father's collapse.

CHARLEY AND BERNARD: These good neighbors are notable in the play for having traits that contrast strikingly with those of the Lomans. Unlike Willy, Charley lays no claim to greatness. He goes along calmly and quietly, undistinguished but relatively content. His salvation, he declares, is that he never took any interest in anything. That, of course, is not literally true for he shows unusually generous consideration of Willy. But he obviously never developed with Bernard any such intense relationship as existed between Willy and Biff. He set himself a modest goal and is satisfied with modest achievements.

Bernard is no match physically for the athletic Loman boys, and neither he nor his father can work so well with their hands. Bernard, however, studies hard, gets good grades, and despite Willy's disparaging predictions is clearly forging ahead. At the time of Willy's breakdown, he has a wife and two sons and is pleading a fairly big law case before the Supreme Court in Washington. When Willy observes wonderingly that Bernard does not brag, Charley says that his son does not have to—his deeds speak for themselves.

Curiously enough, although opposite in temperament to the Lomans, Charley and Bernard cannot help admiring them. Bernard has no illusions as to the foolishness of Biff's neglect of math. Yet he tries constantly to be of help to him and pleads to carry his helmet or shoulder guards on the day of the big game. Charley, on his part, takes issue with Willy on such vital matters as the importance of being "well liked." Yet it is he who in the end defends Willy to Biff in almost rhapsodic terms. Willy sneered at Charley, insulted him, and then borrowed sizable sums from him. But Charley can say with vehemence, "Nobody dast blame this man."

/

COMMENTARY ON *DEATH OF A SALESMAN*

ESTABLISHED FAME. If *All My Sons* signaled the arrival of Arthur Miller as a most promising young playwright, *Death of a Salesman* raised him to the rank of major American dramatist. Appearing in 1949, only two years after *All My Sons*, it garnered the sought-after Pulitzer Prize, as well as another Critic's Circle Award plus quite a few others. The esteemed critic of the New York *Times*, Brooks Atkinson, called it "one of the finest dramas in the whole range of the American theater," and other leading writers also bestowed high praise. John Gassner saw it as "one of the triumphs of the mundane American stage." Gilbert W. Gabriel described it as a "fine thing, finely done," and Euphemia Wyatt found it a "great American tragedy."

SOCIAL CRITICISM. The play takes issue with those in America who place too much stress upon material gain, at the expense of other, more admirable human values. There are, for instance, several angry comments on the company's callous disregard for the welfare of Willy, who has served it steadily for over thirty years. Linda speaks with anger of his being taken off salary, and both boys think this an outrage. Biff later talks of his father as having "landed in the ash can" and suggests that this is all that a "hard-working drummer" can expect. But the most scathing indictment is actually delivered by means of the portrayal of Howard in the office scene. Howard is so engrossed in his new toy, the mechanical gadget, the tape recorder, that he cannot pay much attention to the human being, Willy. His brusqueness, his impatience, and then his coldly unconcerned notice of dismissal— all support Willy's own contention that the business world has lost all respect, comradeship, and gratitude, and is now merely "cut and dried." The picture, as so often in Miller plays, is not wholly bleak. Charley, after all, is a fairly successful businessman who behaves with very human generosity. But the discharging of Willy is still a harsh commentary on all who think of men only as income-producing machines, those who, as Willy says, will "eat the orange and throw the peel away."

Yet there is also a more general criticism of American values. Willy loves his sons and wants what is best for them. Yet his one insistent message to them is that they must rise rapidly in the business world, outshine all others, and be satisfied only with a fortune like Uncle Ben's. In the first place, there is no guarantee that mere wealth and high position would prove that rewarding. Happy's merchandise manager is clearly not ecstatic even with fifty-two thousand a year, a very good annual income in 1949 or even now. Apart from this, however, there is no indication that either the Loman boys or their father possess the skills necessary to command that kind of return. And this combination of an unfeasible objective and limited talents leads to unfortunate consequences. Rather than be forced to endure the stigma of failure, all three constantly lie about their achievements. But the bragging never wholly downs their feelings of inadequacy. Their second escape route is to dream up dazzling get-rich-quick schemes and coast for a while on the glorious prospects. Yet sooner or later, such bubbles inevitably burst.

In addition, this undue concern over material success breaks down the bonds between men that form the basis for a smooth-functioning society. And as a playwright, Arthur Miller develops as a major theme in many of his works the need for a greater sense of mutual responsibility. When, however, the one desirable goal is to get ahead of everybody else, then the spirit of helpfulness declines. Happy regards his fellow employees as "common" and "petty" or "pompous" and "self-important," and proceeds to ruin their fiancées. Accurately or otherwise, he suggests that this type of discreditable behavior may result from "an overdeveloped sense of competition." What Biff hated most about the business world was always having "to get ahead of the next fella." Ben's lesson to Biff about never fighting fair in the jungle thus seems curiously appropriate. And we note that Willy seems always to think it necessary to dispraise Charley and Bernard, possibly, as Charley suggests, because he has always been jealous.

In viewing America, then, Miller would have less emphasis upon moneymaking as the one criterion of a man's worth and less jungle-style competition. A third criticism is directed against an American tendency to play up the superficial. This is brought out by the excessive fuss over the football game. When Charley asks Willy, who is rushing around with pennants, when he is going to grow up, the question is probably more general than it seems. Then there is Howard's playing with his tape recorder, a gadget that so fascinates him now that he is ready to throw out his camera, bandsaw, and other toys. In like manner in the restaurant scene the talk is of French champagne, magazine cover girls, pro-football stardom—all automatically impressive. And those who play tennis and have a swimming pool are, without question, "fine people" to Willy. A society, in Miller's opinion, so given to frivolous judgments, reveals rather distorted values.

POLITICAL BEARINGS. The United States is largely an industrial nation, and its economic system is based on free enterprise and considerable competition. Some of those who are proud of the American way of life object to the type of critical approach taken in such a play as *Death of a Salesman*. Their feeling is that, in showing a "little man" like Willy so callously discharged after long years of service, the whole system is being attacked. In opposition to this viewpoint several arguments have been advanced. First of all, Willy himself is hardly represented as completely typical. Arthur Miller once noted that average men don't commit suicide. Secondly, Willy is not altogether an innocent victim. Part of his difficulty results from family tensions rather than defects in the system. Thirdly, the system seems to operate fairly enough for Charley and Bernard, both of whom are sympathetic characters. Finally, political terms are not used. In other words, there is never any suggestion that some other existing system would be preferable, nor is there any linking of Willy's downfall with some readily identifiable policy of some party or group. Miller is an intellectual much concerned about what he regards as certain defects in our society. His dramas doubtless have general political implications, but almost never do they contain explicit references or recommendations.

MODERN TRAGEDY. Again, as in *All My Sons,* Miller deals with middle-class people in an often quite realistic setting. The salesman's house is in Brooklyn, and the big game takes place at Ebbets Field. The Lomans have owned a Studebaker and a Chevrolet, and wish they had bought a General Electric refrigerator. The restaurant is on West 48th Street, and Happy boasts that Biff is a quarterback with the New York Giants.

As for the strictly tragic element, apart from the previously noted social criticism in the Ibsen tradition, this is, first of all, a play about a man's death. And tragedy has from the beginning dealt with this awesome experience, regarding it as significant and moving. Yet most early tragedies included a great reversal of fortunes, in which a great or powerful person fell to his ruin from a high position of wealth and authority. Here, at the start of the play, Willy is already broken and was never an influential or famous individual. Even the loyal Linda admits that he has never been a "great man" or even the "finest" of characters. Nevertheless, she maintains that he is worthy of some attention as a human being who suffers. After all, "a small man can be just as exhausted as a great man." Willy, for all this ordinariness, has rather lofty aspirations for himself and his sons. His goals may not be altogether admirable. But, then, were those of Macbeth and such tyrant heroes of earlier tragedies? Yet Willy pursues them with passionate intensity. He wants his flawed concept of success with a terrible earnestness and even dies in quest of his dream. Viewed in one way, Willy is a pathetic, incompetent old drummer with absurd pretensions. Miller sees him, however, as aiming high and agonizing deeply. Hence, the "fall" of even such a poor, debt-ridden man can have genuine tragic aspects.

If the play thus contains a new type of tragic statement, it is also curiously lyrical in tone. While this is not poetic drama in the old sense, the preoccupation with the past often gives it a nostalgic, or elegiac, quality. All the Lomans look back a little sadly to happier days of untroubled comradeship when Willy capably directed his sons in carpentry projects for the home. Willy can remember, too, when the business world had in it an element of respect and gratitude. And he can look further back to wagon trips through the developing West. There once was a time, too, when the little house was not jammed in among tall apartment buildings and when Biff waved to Willy from the football field, a young Hercules with the sun all around him. The delicate flute music that hauntingly plays now and then and even the leafy green effect of the lights upon the "fragile-seeming" house add still further to the lyrical effect. *Death of a Salesman* is thus not only a drama of social criticism and a modern tragedy but also a mood piece, wistfully looking back.

EXPERIMENTAL FORM.   As contrasted with *All My Sons,* this play has a much more creative and original format. Miller is attempting to recreate what goes on in Willy's troubled mind. Actually, he once thought of calling the play "The Inside of His Head," and having all scenes played behind a thin curtain, or scrim. Although this proposal was abandoned as unfeasible, the action does move easily back and forth from past to present. Yet, unlike mere accounts of the past, the flashbacks are in a sense part of the present action. For when the distracted Willy is reminded of the disastrous Boston episode, he relives it, goes through it again, and this new, decidedly present experience adds to his current difficulties. Again when he, in a sense, holds a double conversation with Ben from the past and Charley in the present, it is all part of what is going on in his brain here and now. In general, this startling technique was very much admired. According to Miller, it was also imitated, usually by those who had no real grasp of its proper use. It is also interesting that the playwright returned to more conventional forms in subsequent works, only to revive this method in modified form in *After the Fall.*

CHARACTERISTIC THEMES

SELF-DESTRUCTION: As in *All My Sons,* the leading character meets a violent death by his own hands. In both, too, it is a father who kills himself because of a situation in which his sons have judged him harshly.

EXCESSIVE PERSONAL INVOLVEMENT: In both *All My Sons* and *Death of a Salesman*, fathers and sons are concerned about each other's actions to an extreme degree. Larry in *All My Sons* hears of his father's guilt and kills himself, and Chris considers refusing to marry Ann. In *Death of a Salesman* the discovery of his father's secret love affair puts an end to all of Biff's college ambitions. And Willy's yearning for Biff's success finally helps motivate his suicide.

UNETHICAL PRACTICES TO KEEP UP WITH COMPETITION. Keller in *All My Sons* let the defective parts be shipped to save his business. Willy countenances Biff's cheating on exams and his stealing of the football, passing such actions off as examples of initiative.

NEED FOR UNCOMPROMISING INTEGRITY. Chris Keller tries to make his father realize the moral implications of his decision to ship the parts. Biff Loman works to make Willy recognize how much has been false in their lives so that both may make a new start.

SYMBOLS. Certain objects are used in this play to represent significant aspects of the Loman family's experience.

THE FLUTE: The light, elusive melody of the flute recalls earlier, more carefree days. It suggests the wagon trips of Willy's flute-maker father when there was more freedom and opportunity for a man who could work with his hands.

HOUSE AND APARTMENTS: The big new apartment buildings hemming in the Loman home and making it impossible for plants to grow in their backyard are evidence of the social and economic changes occurring in an America that is becoming increasingly urban. Willy is an excellent carpenter, and his sons are husky and virile. But none of them seems to fit in well with the indoor skills now most in demand.

DIAMONDS. These precious stones, which Ben brought out of the jungle, signify at least to Willy hard, tangible evidence of success. There is also beauty in them which appeals to his somewhat romantic nature. Pawning the diamond watch fob for Biff's correspondence course indicates his love for his son. And when he finally settles on a suicide course to get the insurance money, he sees this as a diamond "shining in the dark."

MISCELLANEOUS. *Cars:* Polishing the car was one of the happiest memories in Willy's life; he now uses his car to re-establish this time of promise by leaving the money to Biff. *Stockings:* The showy gesture of stockings given to the buyer viewed in contrast to Linda's day-to-day darning is quite apparent to the shocked younger Biff. *Tape recorder:* Howard's concern for machines more than for men. *Tennis rackets:* symbols of Bernard's enviable success.

REVIEW QUESTIONS AND ANSWERS

1. Much of *Death of a Salesman* deals with the relationship between Willy and Biff. Could Happy have been eliminated?

ANSWER: No, for Happy is useful in providing a perspective by which the other two can be more accurately evaluated. Happy is reasonably open-handed. He will treat his father to dinner, even send him to Florida, and pledge more, if necessary. But he was never the favorite and was never caught up in the terrible disillusioning experience of Biff. For that matter, except in a general, vague fashion, Willy never seems to have expected too much from this younger son. Yet Happy has learned from his father. He has been taught the necessity of pushing to the top, of sneering at superiors and coworkers, and of not being scrupulous about an unethical practice or two. He is also an expert at bluffing, and lies almost instinctively whenever unpleasant truths threaten to prove irksome. Being harder than Willy and Biff, he has been able to work out a somewhat more satisfactory compromise. He has, after all, his car, his apartment, and his women friends, whereas both his father and his brother have almost no funds. He does have twinges of conscience but lets no troublesome sense of guilt interfere with his sensual pleasures. When Biff brings up some agonizing truths, he angrily denies them, preferring the tried and serviceable lie. Yet Willy and Biff are more poetic, more romantic, more akin to the old visionary pioneers. They love more and suffer more. And Biff may even achieve some measure of maturity. Happy has taken the worst of Willy's precepts and made them his life's code. As a character, he enables us to see Willy's errors in action. He also makes us appreciate the greater moral sensitivity of the other two Loman men.

2. If Willy's character is clearly a foolish, headstrong one, are we to assume that Charley and Bernard represent the playwright's ideal?

ANSWER: This we can assume only to a limited extent. Certainly Charley and Bernard seem to have more serene, more comfortable lives than the Lomans. Bernard has a wife and two sons, and his career is obviously thriving. His father can afford to lend Willy substantial sums, to have his own secretary, and to present a bottle of bourbon to the departing Bernard. Even with Willy in a sadly distraught condition, Charley can offer him a job. Moreover, the relationship between this father and son is friendly and untroubled. Hence, almost no negative side can be seen to their lives. And, by inference, the Lomans would be happier, more truly successful were they able to conform to the steadier, more easy-going life patterns of their neighbors.

Yet there is something heroic in the very aspirations of the Lomans. Willy speaks of his father as an "adventurous man" and talks of a "little streak of self-reliance" in his family. Willy may be born in the wrong era for his type of skills. But he does have some vestiges of the old pioneering vision, the boundless optimism, the reckless element that was part of America's heritage. Why does Charley keep coming around despite the insults? Why does young Bernard slave patiently for Biff? Neither can or will adopt the Lomans' dangerous course, but both sense here a bit of excitement, a flash of glory absent in their well-regulated lives. Like most of the far-from-sensible heroes of other eras, the Lomans live more perilously and risk more. But even failing, they are the dreamers that rescue civilization from becoming too drearily cut and dried.

3. What dramatic purpose is served by using flashbacks instead of relating events in strict chronological order?

ANSWER: The flashback scenes in *Death of a Salesman* differ from those in many other works. Ordinarily the flashback device is used primarily for exposition, that is, to convey background information needed to make the story as a whole intelligible. Of course, the scenes from the past in this play do indeed fulfill such a purpose. The episode in the Boston hotel, for instance, explains certain of the quarrels between Willy and Biff and accounts for Willy's sense of guilt. Yet such episodes also serve here another, more subtle purpose.

Willy Loman, the hero, will die at the end of the play not from old age, a dread disease, or a sniper's bullet, but in a suicidal car crash. He will kill himself because painful memories, guilt feelings, and various frustrations combine to unsettle his mind and distort his thinking. The flashbacks here are scenes from the past that torment and confuse Willy in the present. Pleasant recollections make him more agonizingly conscious of current sorrows. Disturbing ones reinforce the anxieties of the moment. Used in this fashion, episodes from Willy's past are very much a part of his later experience and, in a way, are just as essential to the main action as his crucial final encounters with Howard and Biff.

Finally, since this is to some extent a psychological drama, what

Willy's confused mind instinctively recalls tells us a great deal about the kind of man he is. Would Charley, for instance, remember the football game so vividly? Thus the flashbacks here not only provide exposition but advance the plot and reveal character traits.

4. Why has Willy Loman seemed to many an unusual choice for the hero of a tragedy?

ANSWER: Tragedy as a type of drama was first successfully developed by such ancient Greek playwrights as Aeschylus, Sophocles, and Euripides. Many of our traditional concepts of tragedy derive from their handling of the form and from the commentary on their works provided by the philosopher Aristotle. The Greek tragic hero was in some respects quite different from Willy Loman.

First of all, the Greek hero was usually at the start of a play a man in an extremely fortunate position. Oedipus, for instance, is the rich and respected ruler of a state, enjoying good health, peace of mind, and the contentment of a satisfactory home life. By contrast, Willy starts as a broken, exhausted, confused "little man," bitterly at odds with his eldest son. The Greek hero fell from an exalted position, and much of the tragedy consisted in the appalling extent of his decline. But Willy has never far to fall.

Secondly, the Greek hero, although not a perfect man, seemed to sum up man's nobler aspirations. Some have felt that Willy's values are so warped and his vision so limited that he cannot qualify as a noble example of mankind. The lordly warrior Agamemnon, they maintain, would not fret about being "well liked" or get so worked up over a football game. To this Arthur Miller has replied that even poor, confused man can want with passionate intensity a sort of distinction for himself and his son, and that if he wants this enough to die for it, he achieves tragic status. Not all have accepted his contention. But some agree that since our civilization is not that of ancient Greece, our tragic hero will perhaps differ too.

5. What purposes are served by the flute music used throughout *Death of a Salesman?*

ANSWER: From the first the flute is used to create a mood or an atmosphere. Even though Willy is a heavy-set, aging man, lumbering in with weighty valises, he is also an individual forever pursuing an elusive vision or dream. And the light music of the flute, never pronounced or intrusive, keeps this side of Willy before the audience.

It is also used to provide transitions from present-day scenes to flashbacks and vice versa. Unlike many more conventional works, this play does not lower any curtain as the action moves from one place to the other, or even from one moment in time to another that occurred fifteen years before. The flute is used to smooth over the frequent shifts and to help set successive scenes.

Thirdly, the flute is connected with Willy's family history. His father, that great, "wild-hearted" man, made flutes and took his family in a wagon all over the country selling them. He was thus a craftsman, and Willy is always proud of being able to do things with his hands. He was also, of course, a salesman, and his roving, "adventurous" life has obviously signified to Willy a type of free, unencumbered existence, with profits unlimited for those who can quickly invent some such clever gadget. The sound of the flute is thus also the call Willy never wholly stops hearing to a challenging nomadic career, probably in the great West.

6. Indicate several criticisms directed in *Death of a Salesman* against contemporary American society.

ANSWER: First of all, the play suggests that modern business is so coldly competitive that decent human values are ignored. Willy gives many years of steady service to the Wagner Company. As soon, however, as his production begins to decline, he is taken off salary and put back on straight commission. Then, subsequently, he is discharged, apparently without any pension or other means of income. In addition, both Biff and Happy talk of business conditions in terms that suggest that competition encourages sharp practice or outright dishonesty.

Secondly, the work takes issue with exaggerated emphasis upon personal charm rather than upon more solid character traits. Willy keeps telling Biff that it is all important to be well liked. Biff can fail subjects and even steal with impunity provided that he has a winning smile and an attractive manner. Actually, Biff's poor grades deprive him of scholarships, and because of his lack of other necessary skills he never makes high wages. And despite his likable personality, theft still draws him a jail term.

Thirdly, the drama seems to hint that too much stress upon certain types of white-collar work has driven those into it who would be better off working with their hands. And in general, the over-all worship of material success is seen to produce in some instances little more than a sense of failure and frustration.

7. Although *Death of a Salesman* is not poetic drama in the usual sense, it does seem to many to have a lyrical, elegiac quality, as the

characters look back with sadness to happier times. What evidence is there of this lament for the past?

ANSWER: Willy Loman, when the play opens, is old, exhausted, and incapable of meeting the demands of his job. So he tends to recall a period some fifteen years earlier when life was much more pleasant. He was making more money then, and the old red Chevrolet shone, thanks to Biff's expert polishing. Biff was the popular captain of his high school football squad and was playing in a championship game. Furthermore, Biff then had excellent prospects. Three universities were making overtures about athletic scholarships. Above all, Willy was then idolized by both his boys, and peace and harmony reigned in the family.

Apart from Willy's own personal life, however, other changes have been occurring. When the Lomans first moved to Brooklyn, there were small houses and pleasant flower and vegetable gardens. The light and air were good for the spirit, and the chance for a man to plant and build increased his self-respect. Now, however, tall apartment buildings surround the small home, and, by implication, the small man. He can no longer grow vegetables or smell the flowers. He feels stifled, trapped.

In addition, the business picture has changed. There is more of the coldly mechanical even in sales transactions, whereas formerly, as when old Dave Singleton flourished, there was more evidence of respect, comradeship, and gratitude.

8. Why does Charley once remark that Willy really is a salesman and does not know it?

ANSWER: So far as Willy's actual achievements as a representative for the Wagner Company are concerned, it is hard to evaluate his record. Linda tends to flatter him, Howard is too ready to deny all his claims, and Willy himself rarely offers reliable facts about his work. Chances are, however, that at least in his prime, Willy was at least as good as the next man. He has, after all, held the job over the years. And he does support his family except for the final few months and pay off the mortgage on his house. As opposed, for example, to the Carbone family in *A View from the Bridge*, who live in a crowded tenement, the Lomans do manage to acquire property.

Yet Willy, however ordinary or average is his work for the company, is an expert at "selling" himself certain rather dubious notions. He is forever bragging about his popularity in New England and seems convinced that many will come from other states to his funeral. He is certain that Biff, having played a good game of football, will outshine everyone in the business world. And later he is certain that Oliver will lend Biff a sizable sum although his son can offer no security. At the end, he talks himself into the belief that his suicide will somehow enable Biff to take the lead once more from Bernard and become at once "magnificent." Charley's wry comment in the "Requiem," seems to take into account this astonishing facility Willy has for persuading himself and even others to buy unlikely possibilities.

9. Is there some suggestion here that both Willy and Biff are too emotionally concerned about each other's way of life?

ANSWER: Charley tries more than once to get Willy to let Biff alone to work out his own problems. After all, Biff is a man thirty-four years old. But Willy cannot heed this advice, even though he is impressed with the way Charley's hands-off policy has worked with the increasingly successful young Bernard.

Willy sees Biff's failure to settle down in some career as a spite campaign directed against him personally. Ever since Biff found him in a compromising situation in Boston, he has felt guiltily uneasy, afraid that he may inadvertently have blighted Biff's life. Yet, unwilling to admit such responsibility, he tries to blame Biff, accusing him of taking a mean and excessive revenge. Yet Willy has so identified his own interests with those of Biff that he still wants to "give him something." When Biff mentions the Oliver scheme, Willy nervously loads him with instructions as to how to behave. And once convinced of Biff's affection, Willy prepares to kill himself to give Biff the insurance money.

For his part, Biff has worries about his lack of material success that probably have nothing to do with Willy. Yet his sense of having proved a terrible disappointment to his father weighs him down further, and also stirs up defensive anger against Willy as the "fake" who let him down first. Both are grown men, in theory able to handle their own affairs. Yet both, because of strong guilt feelings, can neither achieve a mature, friendly relationship, nor let go and work out their personal problems alone.

10. How does Biff in *Death of a Salesman* compare with Chris in *All My Sons* as a key character?

ANSWER: Both young men begin by idolizing their fathers and later denounce them furiously. Chris astonished Ann and others by the extent to which he admires Joe. Yet, when he discovers Keller's part in shipping the defective materials, he is calling him the most derogatory names he can imagine. If Willy Loman's memories are at all reliable, Biff, as a high school senior, regarded

Willy with astonishing hero worship. He missed him all the time Willy was away and longed to travel through New England with him. Yet at the end, unable to bear his father's taunts any longer, Biff turns on him and rejects both the man and his teachings.

Of the two, Chris starts with fewer feelings of insecurity. Chris has a good war record, likes his work at the plant, and enjoys the love of a charming and intelligent childhood sweetheart. Hence, Chris at the end can be more the stern and unforgiving accuser than Biff. And indeed Chris does seem to represent more the voice of outraged, decent individuals who discover perfidy and betrayal.

Biff, on the contrary, is poor, jobless, and discouraged. Because his disillusionment regarding Willy occurred years ago, he has had time to develop some feelings of compassion. So his outburst, provoked by Willy's unreasonable attacks, is more defensive and, in a sense, curative than severely denunciatory. And at the end Biff sobs exhaustedly, and Willy recognizes his true affection. Ironically, though, however different are their sons' rejection speeches, both fathers feel impelled to commit suicide.

ALL MY SONS
(1947)

CHARACTERS

JOE KELLER—A small-town factory owner in his late fifties, a solid-looking, slow-speaking, self-made man who places the interests of his immediate family above all other claims.

KATE KELLER—His wife, a few years younger, a loving mother and good neighbor fanatically determined to shield her husband from the consequences of a dishonorable wartime business decision that brought death to U. S. airmen.

CHRIS KELLER—Their sole surviving son, thirty-two, a serious, idealistic young war veteran, now an executive in his father's plant, who hopes to marry Ann Deever.

ANN DEEVER—A pleasant, unassuming, but spirited girl of twenty-six, the daughter of Joe's imprisoned former partner, previously engaged to the Kellers' younger son, Larry (declared missing in action during World War II), but now deeply in love with Chris.

GEORGE DEEVER—Ann's brother, a humane, high-principled young lawyer in his early thirties, morally outraged by what he considers the betrayal of his family by the Kellers.

DR. JIM BAYLISS—The Kellers' next-door neighbor, a fairly successful young doctor who, inspired by Chris, would like to dedicate his life to research, were it not for his wife who insists that he make a good living for his family.

SUE BAYLISS—His wife, fortyish and overweight, who regards the Kellers, and especially Chris, as a threat to her security in that they distract her husband from the lucrative business of calling upon wealthy patients.

FRANK LUBEY—Another neighbor, about as old as Chris and George, a settled nonveteran with three children, who tries to be friendly and helpful and works out horoscopes as a hobby.

LYDIA LUBEY—His young, happy-go-lucky, scatter-brained wife, whom George Deever once thought of marrying before he went to war.

BERT—A lively eight-year-old youngster, who amuses Joe Keller by pretending to be a detective and asking to see the "jail" in the Keller basement.

THE SETTING.   All scenes take place in the middle-class sub-urban backyard of the Keller home. Characters enter and leave the house by the porch door to the rear. In the foreground, to the right is the stump of a small apple tree, blown down by a violent night storm. The month is August, presumably in about the year 1947, when the play first appeared.

PLOT ANALYSIS: ACT I.   On an August Sunday morning, factory owner Joe Keller sits chatting with neighbors Dr. Jim Bayliss and Frank Lubey. They observe that a storm the night before toppled the small apple tree planted in memory of Joe's son Larry, declared missing in action three years ago in the Far East. Lubey announces that he is preparing, at Mrs. Keller's request, a horoscope to determine whether Larry's plane went down on a "favorable" day according to the stars. Kate Keller still passionately denies that her son is dead and seeks a positive sign from astrology.

Stout, sharp-tongued Sue Bayliss drops over, demanding that her husband pay more heed to patients with money. After her comes young, lighthearted Lydia Lubey, bidding her Frank come help her fix the toaster. Before leaving, the neighbors talk briefly of newly arrived Ann Deever, whose family used to occupy the next-door Bayliss home. She has come now to visit the Kellers.

Chris Keller, thirty-two and serious, joins his father, and both watch amused as Bert, a small boy, runs in playing detective to report to Joe as his "chief." Then Chris, troubled, tells Keller that Kate cried bitterly when the tree fell. He insists that his father must make her admit Larry's death. He intends to marry Ann, and wants no talk of stealing his brother's girl. Joe obvious-ly does not relish upsetting his wife further, but Chris threatens to move from town unless his mother agrees to his engagement. This ultimatum greatly disturbs Keller, whose one hope has been to leave his thriving business to his sole surviving son.

Kate Keller enters and jokes with Joe but later complains of an unusual headache. She refers often to Larry, arguing that Ann, his fiancée, would long since have married had she, too, not known he was still living. When Chris objects to such a notion, Kate warns both him and Joe never to stop expecting Larry's return. If he is not coming back, she will kill herself.

Ann comes out, radiantly lovely, and is reservedly welcomed by Kate, especially when the girl makes it clear that she has accepted Larry's death and has ceased to mourn him. They ask about her father, Joe's former partner now in prison because of a wartime business scandal. The Keller plant had shipped cracked cylinder heads for planes to the Army, and twenty-one P-40s crashed. Ann bears no grudge against Joe, who was legally exonerated, but she and her lawyer brother, George, have bitterly renounced their own father, who was convicted. Joe, however, claims that the neighborhood has forgotten old hostilities. He also reminds her how great were governmental pressures during the war, and urges her to relent. Her father was not responsible for Larry's death. He erred but was no murderer.

Alone afterwards with Chris, Ann remarks how unique is Chris's devotion to Joe. She then admits her love for Chris and asks why he took so long to get in touch with her. He explains that upon returning from combat, the sole survivor of his gallant company, he was appalled to find everyone at home so busy making money. For a time he feared that he himself, in prospering, was betraying his fallen comrades. Now, however, he is eager to marry her.

Humorously interrupting their embrace, Keller comes out to announce an unexpected call for Ann from her brother, who has finally been to see their father in prison. Uneasily Joe speculates about Ann's possible resentment and offers to sign over his plant to Chris, who is naturally somewhat alarmed. Learning that George, very much excited, is coming to join Ann, Kate privately warns Joe to use his head. He retorts angrily that he has nothing to fear, but he is clearly quite worried.

ACT II.   Later that day Chris saws off the tree stump, and his mother readies a grape drink that George liked in happier times. She quietly asks Chris to protect his parents, and urges him to let Ann depart with George. Later Ann, out there alone, meets Sue Bayliss. Sue urges Ann to leave town with Chris after their marriage. Her complaint is that Chris's own seeming idealism inspires her husband's dream of giving up his steady practice to be an ill-paid research man. Yet all the while the same hypocritical Chris lives on his father's tainted money! Ann, much disturbed by her hostility, later relays her accusations to Chris. He admits that some do think his father guilty, but he does not. If Joe were culpable, Chris would never forgive him.

Joining them, Joe reveals his limited schooling by not knowing the meaning of "roué" and mispronouncing "brooch." Goodnaturedly, however, he points out that he bosses many former military officers. Suprisingly, he then suggests that Ann's brother might like, with his help, to start a practice in town. He would also take the elder Deever back into the business. Again he urges Ann to forgive him, too, since "a father is a father." At that point, Jim Bayliss arrives, quite uneasy. George is outside in a furious mood, having come to take his sister home.

Despite his own nostalgic feelings for the old neighborhood, George says that Ann cannot marry Chris, since it was Joe who destroyed their family. Having visited his imprisoned father, George is now convinced that Keller actually ordered him by phone to ship the defective parts. Having leveled his accusation, George is again momentarily softened by the arrival of Kate, whom he always liked, and Lydia Lubey, whom he once thought of marrying. And his new faith in his father is further shaken when an unyielding Keller recalls earlier lapses of his erstwhile partner. Then a casual reference to Keller's health prompts Kate proudly to assert that her husband has not been sick in years. This quickly rouses the suspicions of Ann and Chris, as well as George, for Keller was allegedly home with the flu when Deever shipped out the cylinder heads.

At this crucial moment Frank Lubey enters with the horoscope, indicating that Larry disappeared on a "favorable day," when he could not possibly have been killed. Kate then tries to send away George and Ann, but Ann has no wish to leave Chris. Kate then says that either Larry is alive or Joe killed him.

Alone with his father, Chris angrily accuses him. Keller denies being a murderer. He did not think that the defective parts would ever be used and anyway he had intended to warn the authorities. His only thought had been to save the business for his sons. Chris turns on him. How could he kill like that? Has he no country? Does he live in the world at all?

ACT III. At two the next morning, Kate waits up for Chris, who drove off anguished after confronting Joe. Jim Bayliss, who admits that he has long known their secret, reassures her that her son will return and compromise. He himself once ran off to New Orleans to starve as a research scientist but was coaxed back by a tearful Sue. Kate later urges Joe to admit his guilt and, throwing himself on Chris's mercy, even offer to go to prison. Angered in turn, Joe says that she and Chris both wanted money and should not blame him for getting it for them. He did it for his family. If there is anything bigger than his family, he will kill himself.

Ann joins them, promising to remain silent about Joe if Kate will admit Larry's death to Chris. When she is refused, Ann privately shows Kate a letter that shocks the older woman deeply. Returning then, Chris announces that this being the "land of the great big dogs," he too will turn practical. He will leave town without turning his father in. He even coldly admits that his father is no worse than most. He, Chris, simply expected more from him. Afraid of losing him, Ann hands Chris the letter his mother hoped she would suppress. This is Larry's last message. Having read overseas of the initial conviction of his father and Deever, he writes that he cannot bear to go on living and indicates that he will kill himself.

Humbled and broken, Joe finally sees that the boys in the war were all his sons and agrees to go with the implacable Chris to confess to the police. Chris declares that all must be better and admit that they have responsibilities to others. After Joe goes into the house, a shot is heard. Keller has killed himself. Chris says that this was not what he wanted. Kate, however, comforts him, sobbing, and tells him to go on and live.

ANALYSES OF MAJOR CHARACTERS

JOE KELLER: A vigorous, heavy-set man approaching sixty, Joe Keller is proud of his hard-won success in the rough, competitive world of American business. Having been thrust out to work at age ten, with only one later year of night school, he is aware that he lacks the polish provided by education. Yet he is not overly dismayed. Shrewd and resourceful, he knows that in his factory he bosses many college men, even former majors and colonels of World War II. His most rewarding achievement has been providing well for his family. His wife can hire a maid. He can take visitors out to dinner with steak and champagne. Above all, he has built up "one of the best shops in the state" to leave to his son, Chris.

When first encountered on a summer Sunday, at ease in the backyard of his comfortable home, he seems a good-natured, easygoing average citizen. He has a loyal wife, whom he amiably teases, and an admirable son who idolizes him. He gets along well with the neighbors, even losing to them cheerfully at the regular Saturday night poker games in his arbor. He plays detective games with youngsters from the block, saving badges for them from cereal boxes. And he jokes genially, if a bit crudely, with the pretty girl his son hopes to marry. He modestly denies being "brainy," and reads with interest the want ads rather than the news. But he thinks of himself as a "respected man," and, as Ann says, "wants everybody happy." As such, he can ask Chris, with ironic sincerity, "How could I kill anybody?"

As a factory owner, however, this friendly, likable man can be hard and ruthless. Business to him is a war in which personal survival is the prime consideration. Invariably the last to leave his shop, he keeps a close check on all operations, even clocking the time workers spend in lavatories. In his view a good man is one who makes money to support his family. Thus virtually any move he finds it necessary to make to protect this income is to him automatically justified, even if someone outside his family group may thereby suffer grievously. Again, he "wants everybody happy," but if there is a forced choice, "nothin' is bigger" than the family.

During World War II his factory can stay open and the family support be assured only if he can fulfill and retain government contracts. Then by mischance, more than one hundred cylinder heads, destined for fighter planes, prove defective. Not eager to "kill anybody," Joe might not chance sending them out were his government contacts willing to wait for replacements. But if they must either get the parts now or close down his plant, they will get the parts, however unsafe, and he will cope with consequences later. As further family protection, he sets up his weaker, less competent partner and next-door neighbor as scapegoat to bear the blame, should discovery occur before he can straighten matters out. Actually this brings potential disaster extremely close to home, for Deever's daughter is engaged to his soldier son, Larry. But the Deevers are. not yet "family." So, if necessary, they are still expendable.

The play's action takes place three years after the parts scandal made headlines. The war is over. Deever is still in prison; but Joe, again prospering, suffers no obvious twinges of conscience. When, however, old charges are revived, this time within the family, his response is characteristically defiant. "The only way you lick'em is guts!" sums up his attitude. Fighting all the way, he flatly denies all guilt and resolutely quashes all doubts as to his partner's sole responsibility. At the same time, he cannily urges all to regard the culprit with understanding and compassion, hoping for similar magnanimity should the dreaded truth emerge. He is not above bribery, either. Once he offers to turn his whole plant over to Chris. He will also generously hold a job for Deever, anticipating the latter's release. He even suggests that Ann's brother, George, might set up a law practice in town, assured of princely support. Even when cornered, he still does battle. For one thing, this was no deliberate murder, merely a human error under extraordinary pressures. For another, Chris and even Kate always were glad to take his money, never closely investigating its source. And, after all, no one "worked for nothin' in that war." So why was he so bad?

Larry's letter, however, does finally destroy his bravado. Realizing that inadvertently he helped bring about his son's death, Keller crumbles. Moreover, he appreciates for the first time Chris's contention that those young men who crashed in planes with the faulty cylinder heads were also in a sense his "sons." He can thus no longer cling to the narrow code which has so long sustained him. Sternly condemned by Chris, he loses heart to begin anew. Taking decisive action for the last time, Joe shoots himself.

Ignorant but crafty, easy-going yet relentless, at once cowardly and aggressive, Keller .is a fairly complex character. If the playwright has not altogether reconciled certain contradictory tendencies in his personality, the rugged factory owner is an impressive creation, at least credible enough to make audiences wonder just how typical his warped values are in contemporary society.

KATE KELLER: Somewhat younger than her husband, Kate is also a study in contrasts. At first glance, she, too, seems a nice, normal middle-class type. She is Mother, good-hearted if a bit peppery, catered to and fussed over by amiably grumbling menfolk. She has also, however, a wild, fanatical streak. In following through a course of action, determined quite arbitrarily, she can be brutally high-handed.

Although Larry has been officially missing for three years, she sternly insists that he is alive and will tolerate no denials. At the outset this may appear simply the pitiable self-delusion of a grieving parent. Back of it, however, is some curious reasoning. Kate all along has known of Joe's crime and has helped him conceal it. There is no hint that she strove to dissuade him and no indication of her being concerned over the Deever conviction. Yet, unlike Joe, she does tormentedly link the plane crashes due to the faulty parts with Larry's disappearance.

She does not, of course, share Chris's vision of an over-all human bond that makes all the young airmen in a sense sons of the Kellers. Even when toward the end she tells Joe, "It don't excuse it that you did it for the family," she seems mainly trying to make him see Chris's point of view so that he can make his peace with the young man. Throughout the play, she herself, like Joe, puts family welfare above all other claims.

She is aware, naturally, as is Joe, that since Larry did not fly a P-40 he could not literally have crashed in one of the planes with cracked cylinder heads. Yet the failure of his plane would represent to her a cruel reprisal taken by an outraged God. Exactly how she arrives at this conclusion is not clear, but she is convinced of but two alternatives. If Larry actually died, then Joe inadvertently but surely "killed" him. If Larry is still alive, then Joe merely made an unfortunate wartime error, and "The war is over."

So Larry must live, for "God does not let a son be killed by his father." She keeps his room always ready and his shoes shined. She hears him calling to her in dreams that seem veritable visions. She casts Ann in the role of faithfully waiting fiancée and regards the fallen tree as a favorable omen. She even begs a horoscope from Frank Lubey, whom she curtly characterizes as a "big dope," in hopes that astrology will support her contention.

Above all, there must be no marriage between Chris and Ann,

"Larry's girl." Kate would not normally be hostile to the younger Deevers. She knew them as small children. Even now she remembers the grape drink George used to like and talks of fattening him up and getting him a wife. But to let Ann marry Chris would be, in her view, admitting Larry's death and calling Joe his son's murderer. This being unthinkable, she makes the girl feel unwelcome, tries speeding her departure, and even officiously packs her bag. The fact that Chris and Ann love each other scarcely bothers her. If Joe would sacrifice others to save a business for his family, she can be equally unsparing to "prove" him innocent of their son's death.

When the letter Ann produces blasts her hopes irrevocably, she still works to protect Joe. Her first thought is to keep him from reading its grim message. Then she tries to reassure him, get him to rest. And meanwhile she keeps on pleading with the adamant Chris. Although she herself has been deeply shocked, her desperate last-ditch effort is still to save her husband. Only after the shot rings out does she turn consoling eyes on Chris.

A passionately loyal wife, Kate takes a bizarre approach to the problem of Keller's guilt. In general, however, her concepts of right and wrong, like her husband's, are a matter of what helps or harms those close to her. At one point Sue Bayliss wryly describes Ann as the "female version" of Chris. Kate may dwell upon mystic signs and portents, whereas Keller has a practical, down-to-earth mentality. Yet essentially she is very much the "female version" of Joe.

CHRIS KELLER: A quiet, thoughtful young veteran, Chris is a confirmed idealist. This is apparent in his attitudes toward the war, the business world, his parents, Ann, and even the neighbors. He has only bitter contempt for those who call it "practical" to prosper through sharp dealings. He hates all forms of moral compromise and scrupulously worries lest he be guilty of it himself.

He identifies World War II strictly with the deaths of brave young fighting men. The company he commanded were gallant, selfless lads who died for a noble cause. And their sacrifices seemed to Chris to herald a new order in which men in general would recognize their responsibilities to all their fellow human beings and be above petty personal considerations.

Painfully conscious of having survived the wiping out of his company, he returns home exalted only to be sadly disillusioned. First of all, Americans on the home front seem to give no thought to his fallen comrades. They are too busy making money. In addition, he sees no evidence of that new spirit of responsibility and mutual assistance that he had so hopefully anticipated. Finally, he encounters serious corruption, such as that exposed when Deever was convicted, and that tempts him to become cynical.

Like his parents, however, he finds temporary peace of mind by focusing on his own family group. Although uneasy for a time because he is making money as are the greedy men he despises, he has the comforting assurance that he is working for his father, who runs a "clean" business. Deever, the villain, has been caught and punished. His Dad, once unjustly accused, has been exonerated. He can, therefore, with a clear conscience live at home for three years as a devoted son, working cheerfully at his father's side, regardless of the neighborhood consensus that Joe "pulled a fast one." To him Keller is a victim, "falsely accused," who has been put "through hell."

According to the rueful Mrs. Bayliss, Chris makes "people want to be better than it's possible to be." Her husband may be a fairly successful doctor, but Chris rouses in him all his early dreams of devoting himself to poorly paid research projects. Totally unaware that Sue Bayliss thinks of him as a hypocritical fraud out to destroy her marriage, he speaks glowingly of her to Ann as a "great nurse." Ann amusedly says he's always finding a "distinction" for everyone, and his mother accuses him of expecting everyone to like him because he goes on liking everybody.

As regards Ann, Chris at first fears that he may be selfishly profiting from his brother's misfortune. Eventually, however, he concludes that he and Ann have a right to marry and asks her home for a visit. Yet he still wants his mother's consent. Her perverse insistence that his brother still lives affects him against his will. He threatens to take Ann and move away if Kate will not relent. But what he wants is, clearly, to go on after marriage keeping those pleasant, comforting contacts with Mom and the "great guy" who is his father.

Chris is never one for halfway measures. He will permit no excuses to be offered for Ann's father. "Kick him in the teeth," he urges Keller, and will hear no talk of rehiring him upon his release. When his own father is accused, he loyally defends him. But once convinced of his father's guilt, he is implacable. Keller's advanced age, his never-ceasing, generous concern for Chris over the years, Kate's impassioned pleas—nothing avails. If Chris is not to despise himself as "practical" or be guilty himself of moral compromise, he must haul Keller promptly off to jail. When Joe desperately contends that he is no worse than most, Chris counters with "I thought you were better."

Although his idealism sets him apart from his parents and from others in his circle, Chris is as hard as Joe was when he double-crossed Deever and as determined as Kate when she undertakes to save Joe. He, too, may normally be loving and affectionate, but let him once encounter unexpected proof of grave failings in those whom he has idolized, and he is merciless. Joe's suicide is all that tempers the terrible wrath of one who so wanted the postwar world to be worthy of all his slain brothers.

ANN DEEVER: This "female version" of Chris is a pleasant, likable young woman with the same flinty toughness noticeable in the Kellers. She loves Chris and, having waited for him long and patiently, has no wish to antagonize his family. Once aware, however, of Kate's hostility, she makes it quite clear that she is not going to be any pawn in the older woman's scheme to keep up the fiction that Larry will return.

She avoids being rude and never panics. Moreover, with admirable restraint, she withholds the crucial letter until forced either to use it or lose Chris altogether. Even then she tries first to shield Joe by handing it to Kate alone.

When her father was convicted, she renounced him with the same brusque finality with which Chris later seeks to dismiss Joe. Curiously enough, she is less severe towards Keller, when the latter's perfidy is revealed. But by that time all she cares about is safeguarding her future with Chris.

When Ann snatches the letter from the protesting Kate and thrusts it into Chris's hands, she is sacrificing the older Kellers just as Joe used her father and Kate tried to separate her from Chris. At this point, Kate, now fully informed, is no longer a threat, but Chris is wavering. Bitterly conscious of how little honor is left in the world, he is tempted to let Keller's crime go unpunished. But if he adopts this "practical" attitude, he will hate himself and be too ashamed to marry Ann. So to make him so incensed that he will have no compunction about turning Joe in to the police and thus keep his own self-respect, Ann deliberately hands him the letter. A gentle, pretty girl, Ann, too, gives no quarter when her marriage hopes are jeopardized. If she shares Chris's idealism, she also duplicates Kate's fierce protectiveness regarding the man she loves.

COMMENTARY ON *ALL MY SONS*

NEW PLAYWRIGHT. In January, 1947, *All My Sons* attracted considerable critical attention. For one thing it introduced to theatregoers a new young American playwright, one with unmistakable creative power. During the previous decade there had been interesting works produced by Maxwell Anderson, John Steinbeck, William Saroyan, and Lillian Hellman, and Tennessee Williams had begun his rise to fame with *The Glass Menagerie.* Still, there were relatively few eminent serious dramatists. O'Neill's most recent offering had been *Ah, Wilderness!* in 1933, and the New York Drama Critics' Circle had skipped awards for best American plays for 1938-39, 1941-42, and 1943-44. Also, no Pulitzer Prize for drama had been given in 1942. So the emergence of Arthur Miller was hopefully regarded, and *All My Sons* won the New York Drama Critics' Circle award for the 1946-47 season.

TEMPER OF THE TIMES. *All My Sons* opened less than two years after Japan's surrender terminated World War II, and some months before peace treaties were signed for Italy and Rumania. During this period the country was changing back to a peacetime economy, and, as is customary after most terrible wars, there was some disillusionment and some questioning as regards the good faith of some participants. Returning veterans, for instance, did sometimes look askance at those on the home front who had prospered during their absence. Hence, Miller's play, with its painful probing of the implications of one minor wartime scandal, seemed to many a unique attempt to come to grips dramatically with certain doubts and anxieties that were disturbing thoughtful Americans.

POLITICAL BEARINGS. Some, it is true, were irritated by what they considered the play's hostile attitude towards American business. Joe, the factory owner, not only ships defective parts to the Army but also angrily defends his action on the grounds that he is no worse than any of the rest who got well paid for guns and trucks. "Who worked for nothin' in that war?" Chris, too, has seen profiteers at home making "suckers" out of gallant soldiers and can refer in a bitter moment to "the land of the great big dogs." On the other hand, it has been pointed out that if Joe is a "bad" businessman, Chris is a "good" one. And we are not necessarily to take as the playwright's personal view what is said by Chris, when roused almost to hysteria, or of Joe who is seizing upon every pretext to defend the indefensible.

MODERN TRAGEDY. As a drama *All My Sons* has often been linked with the plays of the Norwegian Henrik Ibsen. Writing during the second half of the nineteenth century, Ibsen became noted for dramas of social criticism mostly about middle-class characters. And Miller's admiration for his predecessor is evident in his having worked out his own English version of Ibsen's *An Enemy of the People.* In this same tradition, *All My Sons* is a tightly constructed work. Its action occurs in one place (the Keller backyard) and all within one day, thus preserving the "unity of time," used by Ibsen and earlier classical writers. Setting and dialogue are generally realistic, and there are almost no irrelevant lines. Also, as in Ibsen, there is some use of symbols. The grape drink, for instance, recalls happier childhood meetings, and the fallen tree is linked with the death of young Larry.

Above all, as in the deaths of certain Ibsen heroes, this is the tragedy of a not very prominent person. Greek heroes like Oedipus or Agamemnon were usually heads of state. In Shakespeare's time the tragic figure was also a king, such as Lear or Macbeth, or a great general, such as Othello. By comparison, Joe Keller, the owner of a small-town factory, is a "little man." His suicide is not likely to affect much those beyond his immediate circle. Yet Miller sees his fall as significant (1) because he is at least very important to his small group, (2) because he represents, although in somewhat extreme fashion, very real corrupt attitudes in our civilization, and (3) because the very passionate intensity with which he embraces his patently false values gives him tragic stature.

CHARACTERISTIC THEMES. Certain motifs appearing in *All My Sons* recur in later plays by Arthur Miller. Among the more obvious are the following:

VIOLENCE AND SELF-DESTRUCTION: At the conclusion of this play Joe Keller shoots himself following the reading of a letter indicating that his younger son took his own life in World War II. Earlier in the play, Kate, too, has threatened to kill herself. In *Death of a Salesman,* Willy Loman drives his car off the road, but even before this has had some tubing ready as a device for fatally inhaling gas. Again in *After the Fall,* Quentin's friend presumably jumps in front of a subway train, and his second wife seems determined to kill herself with drink and drugs. *The Crucible* and *An Incident at Vichy* both concern mass executions, and *A View From the Bridge* ends with a deadly duel.

PARENT-CHILD CONFLICTS. In this play Joe Keller shockingly disappoints both his sons. Larry kills himself and Chris, who idolized Joe, is appalled and embittered when he learns the truth. Joe, on his part, is crushed when Chris judges him so

severely. In *Death of a Salesman*, Willy is all but worshiped by
Biff until the boy finds out about his shabby affair in Boston.
And Willy, in turn, wants above all to regain the admiration of
his boys. In *The Crucible* John Proctor is vitally concerned about
the name he will leave his children, and Quentin in *After the Fall*
ponders repeatedly certain episodes from his boyhood that were
to affect him later. One he recalls most uneasily is that in which
his mother denounced his father when the latter failed in business.

RESPONSIBILITY TO OTHERS.   Perhaps the most persistent
and most urgent concern in Miller's plays is with man's failure to
act honorably towards his fellows. Joe may be good to his family,
but by allowing defective plane parts to leave his factory he sends
over twenty young airmen to their deaths. Willy in *Death of a
Salesman* wants his sons to be "well liked," but will casually
countenance examination cheating and minor thefts. Quentin, in
After the Fall, does try to assume some responsibility when half-
unwillingly he takes on the legal defense of his accused friend.
And the heroes of both *The Crucible* and *An Incident at Vichy*
finally see their way clear to sacrifice their lives once they recognize their individual responsibilities.

CRITICISMS: Three basic criticisms have been at times leveled
against *All My Sons*. For one thing, some have felt that the dialogue, while it is realistic enough and sounds all right on the stage,
is not as sharp or eloquent as that of the greatest writers. Secondly, some have been distressed by the element of melodrama in
the work. A play, they say, that proposes to treat seriously a problem of values held by average Americans, should be able to do
without such unlikely elements as the two suicides and the curious
romance between members of families so sundered by events.
Finally, there are those who felt that the tightly structured, "well-
made" play in the manner of Ibsen was by 1947 old-fashioned,
and they hoped that in future dramas Miller would experiment
freely. That he agreed was evident in his more imaginative handling
of material in *Death of a Salesman*, which was first presented two
years later, in 1949.

REVIEW QUESTIONS AND ANSWERS

1. Except to provide exposition, or background information, do the Keller neighbors serve any useful dramatic purpose?

ANSWER: In this type of "well-made" play all characters must more than justify their existence or else be discarded. First of all, the Baylisses, the Lubeys, and even little Bert place the Kellers in a community. Miller throughout is much concerned with social bonds, and he wants us to see the Keller family not as isolated but as well-established members of a group. Joe saves cereal-box badges for the youngsters. Jim drives George from the station. Lydia Lubey fixes a hat for Kate. All such close friendly relationships give added weight to Miller's insistence upon responsibility. This one family does not exist alone. It is partially at least dependent upon other families. Hence, Joe's disregard for all others in the interests of his own wife and sons is even more obviously blameworthy.

The neighbors, however, also serve other purposes. Sue Bayliss, for instance, reveals that the community's reacceptance of Joe after the scandal is partially based upon a grudging admiration for a man who can pull a "fast one." On her part, Sue cares nothing for the country's research needs or for her husband's cherished aspirations. She insists that he keep seeing wealthy patients and bring home money. Jim, in turn, assures Kate that all men must compromise, as he has done. Such views effectively point up the frailties of the group that has helped Keller get away with his betrayal for so long. They also throw into sharp relief the genuine and unusual idealism of Chris.

2. At one point Joe Keller claims that he is not "brainy," and Kate tells Chris that both she and his father are "stupid." Is Joe really unintelligent?

ANSWER: Joe Keller has had little formal education. He went to work at ten and after that had only a single year of night school. Yet he is in many ways extremely capable. He ran a substantial plant during the war and rebuilt a thriving business after the scandal that led to his arrest. From the first he was clever enough to set up his weaker partner as scapegoat, and he apparently told a good story to convince the authorities of his innocence. Certainly, the neighbors give him credit for "being smart."

As the play proceeds and the charges are again thrown at him, he again defends himself shrewdly. He skillfully plays up the acknowledged weaknesses in Deever's personality. He carefully plays upon sympathies, anticipating future disclosures, and offers some rather tempting bribes. He is quick to note and try to gloss over Kate's unfortunate slip about his never having been ill, when a bout of flu had been his alibi. And even when the truth is revealed, he so cogently argues that he is merely one among many equally guilty that even the morally outraged Chris momentarily wavers.

Yet in some ways Joe is limited intellectually. He seems actually to have very little concept of a moral code beyond the obligation of a father to pile up wealth for his family. As a result he often seems hopelessly bewildered when Chris talks of his further obligations stemming from his membership in the larger "family" of human beings. In practical matters, Joe is bright and resourceful. When, however, it comes to more complex questions of patriotism and uncompromising integrity, Joe is lost until Larry's letter opens his eyes. But by then it is too late.

3.   Why is *All My Sons* sometimes classified as a social drama?

ANSWER: A social drama is one in which the playwright criticizes certain aspects of the civilization of his own era. Usually it deals with fairly average or typical characters and places them in realistic or recognizable settings. The problems they face are, to some extent, those of ordinary people, and their attitudes toward them are likely to be those that the dramatist observes to be held by people of his generation, or society.

All My Sons deals with Americans living during the years immediately following World War II, and the play actually opened in 1947. At that time, not only the Keller family but many middle-class American families were trying to make the change back to a peacetime economy. And they were beginning to make some judgments about decisions and actions that were hurried through when the war effort was at its peak.

In his play Miller suggests that some Americans on the home front had not kept faith with the men giving their lives on the battlefield. He criticizes the Joe Kellers who thought of business first and patriotism second. And he implies that only if such distorted values are exposed and corrected can the goals for which the terrible war was fought be achieved. Either the spirit of responsibility must be made more universal, or many American sons will have died in vain.

4. What is the dramatic significance of Chris's idealistic tendency always to see people as better than they are?

ANSWER: The play's structure is such that the climactic point
will be Chris's discovery of his father's criminal responsibility in
the shipping of the plane parts. From the start it is established
that Chris has high standards and would never be one to share
in the profits of a business that he thought was tainted by corruption. Chris even hesitated for three years to declare his love
for Ann, lest he in some way be thought to have taken advantage
of his brother's absence from the scene.

Yet it is also important that Chris be not merely stupid or blind.
The neighbors are reasonably sure that Joe has been engaged in
some shady dealing. Yet Chris, who is closest to him, heatedly
denies that his father is guilty. If he is not simply obtuse, then
some other explanation must be offered. So he is described by
Ann as someone who tends to think the best of others.

When the revelation is finally complete, Chris is far more shocked
and more irate than he might be had he been skeptical about
Joe all the time. Hence he can more passionately denounce the
corrupt action, and voice the playwright's own angry criticisms
with more telling force. The tremendous impact upon the loyal
and idealistic Chris of this discovery of betrayal on the part of
the father he had always so admired is thus effective theatre and
effective social criticism.

BIBLIOGRAPHY

PLAYS BY ARTHUR MILLER

After the Fall. New York: Bantam Books, 1965 (paperback).

All My Sons, in *Six Great Modern Plays.* New York: Dell, 1966 (paperback); also in *Collected Plays.*

Collected Plays. New York: The Viking Press, 1958. (Includes *All My Sons, Death of a Salesman, The Crucible, A Memory of Two Mondays,* and *A View from the Bridge.* Also a long, detailed, and helpful Introduction by the playwright.)

The Crucible. New York: The Viking Press, 1953. (Also New York: Bantam Books, 1963 (paperback); and in *Collected Plays.*

Death of a Salesman. New York: The Viking Press, 1964 (paperback); also in *Collected Plays.*

An Enemy of the People. Adapted from Ibsen. New York: The Viking Press, 1951.

Incident at Vichy. New York: The Viking Press, 1965 (paperback).

The Man Who Had All the Luck, in *Cross-Section,* ed. E. Seaver. New York: A. A. Wyn, Inc., 1944.

A Memory of Two Mondays, in *Collected Plays;* and with *A View from the Bridge.* New York: The Viking Press, 1955.

A View from the Bridge, in *Collected Plays;* also, The Viking Press, 1955, and by Bantam Books (paperbacks).

BOOKS WITH BIOGRAPHICAL AND CRITICAL MATERIAL

Atkinson, Brooks. *Broadway Scrapbook.* New York: Theatre Arts, Inc., 1947. (Comments on *All My Sons,* pp. 227-279.)

Bentley, Eric. *In Search of Theatre.* New York: Alfred A. Knopf, 1953. (Comments on *All My Sons,* pp. 32-33, and on *Death of a Salesman,* pp. 84-87.)

Gassner, John. *The Theatre in Our Times.* New York: Crown Publishers, Inc., 1955. (See "New American Playwrights: Williams, Miller, and Others," pp. 342-354, and "Death of a Salesman: First Impressions, 1949," pp. 364-373.)

Heiney, Donald. *Recent American Literature.* New York: Barron's Educational Series, 1958. (Brief biography and studies of principal plays, pp. 400-406.)

Krutch, Joseph Wood. *American Drama since 1918.* New York: G. Braziller, 1957.

Krutch, Joseph Wood. *"Modernism" in Modern Drama.* Ithaca, N. Y.: Cornell University Press, 1953. (Comments on *Death of a Salesman.*)

Lewis, Allan. *American Plays and Playwrights of the Contemporary Theatre.* New York: Crown Publishers, Inc., 1965. (Includes comments on *After the Fall* and *Incident at Vichy* in "Arthur Miller: Return to the Self," pp. 35-52.)

Hurrell, John D., ed. Reviews and criticisms of *Death of a Salesman* from various publications by Atkinson, George Jean Nathan, and others, in *Two Modern American Tragedies.* New York: Charles Scribner's Sons, 1961 (paperback).

Kernodle, George. "The Death of the Little Man," *Tulane Drama Review,* I, (1955-56), 47-60. (Comment on *Death of a Salesman.*)

Miller, Arthur. "Tragedy and the Common Man," *New York Times* (Feb. 27, 1949), sec. 2, pp. 1, 3. (Also in Hurrell, *Two Modern American Tragedies.*)

Miller, Arthur, Richard Watts, John Beaufort, *et al.* "A Matter of Hopelessness in *Death of a Salesman: A Symposium,*" *Tulane Drama Review,* II (May, 1958), 63-69. (Also in Hurrell, *Two Modern American Tragedies.*)

Tynan, Kenneth. "American Blues. The Plays of Arthur Miller and Tennessee Williams," *Encounter,* II (May, 1954), 13-19. (Also in Hurrell, *Two Modern American Tragedies.*)

Whitley, Alvin. "Arthur Miller: An Attempt at Modern Tragedy," *Wisconsin Academy of Sciences, Arts and Letters, Transactions,* XLII (1953), 257-262.

Nannes, Caspar H. *Politics in the American Drama, 1890-1960.* Washington, D. C.: Catholic University Press, 1960.

Sievers, W. David. *Freud on Broadway.* New York: Hermitage House, 1955. (Comments on *All My Sons, Death of a Salesman,* and *The Crucible.)*

Welland, Dennis. *Arthur Miller.* New York: Grove Press, Inc., 1961. (Paperback. Includes biography and comment on *Focus, The Misfits,* and other works, as well as the plays.)

CRITICAL MATERIAL IN PERIODICALS

Couchman, Gordon. "Arthur Miller's Tragedy of Babbitt," *Educational Theatre Journal*, VII (October, 1955), 206-11.

Downer, Alan S. "Mr. Williams and Mr. Miller," *Furioso* (Summer, 1949), pp. 66-70.

Driver, Tom F. "Strength and Weakness in Arthur Miller," *Tulane Drama Review*, IV (May, 1960), 45-52.

Gassner, John. "Tragic Perspectives: A Sequence of Queries," *Tulane Drama Review*, II (May, 1958), 7-22. (Comments on *Death of a Salesman;* also reprinted in Hurrell, *Two Modern American Tragedies*.)

Hunt, Albert. "Realism and Intelligence. Some Notes on Arthur Miller," *Encore*, VII (May-June, 1960), 12-17, 41.

Hurrell, John D., ed. Reviews and criticisms of *Death of a Salesman* from various publications by Atkinson, George Jean Nathan, and others, in *Two Modern American Tragedies*. New York: Charles Scribner's Sons, 1961. (Paperback)

Kernodle, George. "The Death of the Little Man," *Tulane Drama Review*, I (1955-6), 47-60. (Comment on *Death of a Salesman*.)

Miller, Arthur. "Tragedy and the Common Man," *New York Times* (Feb. 27, 1949), Sec. 2, pp. 1,3. (Also in Hurrell, *Two Modern American Tragedies*.)

Miller, Arthur, Richard Watts, John Beaufort, *et al.* "A Matter of Hopelessness in *Death of a Salesman. A Symposium*," *Tulane Drama Review*, II (May, 1958), 63-69. (Also in Hurrell, *Two Modern American Tragedies*.)

Tynan, Kenneth. "American Blues. The Plays of Arthur Miller and Tennessee Williams," *Encounter*, II (May, 1954), 13-19. (Also in Hurrell, *Two Modern American Tragedies*.)

Whitley, Alvin. "Arthur Miller: An Attempt at Modern Tragedy," *Wisconsin Acad. of Sciences, Arts and Letters, Transactions*, XLII (1953), 257-262.

NOTES

NOTES

NOTES

NOTES

NOTES

MONARCH® NOTES AND STUDY GUIDES

ARE AVAILABLE AT RETAIL STORES EVERYWHERE

In the event your local bookseller
cannot provide you with other
Monarch titles you want —

ORDER ON THE FORM BELOW:

Simply send retail price, local sales tax, if any, plus 35¢ per book to cover mailing and handling.

TITLE #	AUTHOR & TITLE	PRICE
	PLUS ADDITIONAL $1.00 PER BOOK FOR POSTAGE	
	GRAND TOTAL	$

Mail to: **PRENTICE HALL PRESS,** c/o Simon & Schuster Mail Order Billing, Route 59 at Brook Hill Drive, West Nyack, NY 10994

I enclose $ .... to cover retail price, local sales tax, plus mailing and handling. (Make checks payable to Simon & Schuster, Inc.)

Name _____
(Please print)
Address _____

City _____ State _____ Zip _____

Please send check or money order. We cannot be responsible for cash.

m

MONARCH NOTES

ARTHUR MILLER'S
DEATH OF A SALESMAN
and All My Sons

- Detailed Plot Summary
- Complete Background
- Character Analysis
- Essay Questions, Model Answers, AND MORE

$3.50

0-671-00688-6

P9-BTS-267